Selected Objectives

for the English Language Arts

Grades 7-12

ARNOLD LAZARUS

Purdue University

ROZANNE KNUDSON

HOUGHTON MIFFLIN COMPANY

BOSTON New York · Atlanta · Geneva, ILL. · Dallas · Palo Alto

Contents

v

Foreword

The field of English as a secondary-school subject may not be character-ized as "new" English in the sense that we have a new math, new sciences, new methods of teaching foreign languages. In some secondary-school English classes we still have the old muddle; in others, the neat, anti-septic, closely packaged course into which teacher and students retreat safely. Nevertheless, English as a school subject is not stagnant, nor its teachers dormant. Extensive changes are developing in all of its aspects. Many teachers welcome these changes and find them liberating in one way or another. But some seem bewildered by them, feeling pressured either to substitute new muddles for old or to withdraw from the commotion entirely.

Probably the most perplexed are English teachers in training, partic-ularly the student teachers and interns who are caught between learning about these developments and concurrently trying to adapt some of them to their classes in secondary schools, sometimes in an environment in-different to the ferment, if not actively hostile. How does a beginner or even an experienced teacher of English find his way among the staples and the multiple and sometimes contradictory new developments in his field?

In this book, Professors Arnold Lazarus and Rozanne Knudson of Purdue University offer extensive help to all teachers of English in public secondary schools, to prospective teachers, and to college and university faculties and supervisors who instruct and consult with teachers of English. From the vast body of literature in the fields of teacher education and of the teaching of English in public secondary schools, and from recom-mendations made by specialists in these fields, they have extracted specific objectives to be achieved by high-school students of English. As the title indicates, the authors do not presume that their objectives are all-inclusive. Nor do they presume to be offering definitive statements of objectives relevant to the teaching of English. Instead, they invite debate and research.

But their lists are detailed, specific, and comprehensive. Here, in one convenient handbook are clear-cut, applicable objectives they believe students should achieve in listening, speaking, reading (including the various forms of literature), reasoning, and writing. And in the appendix they present language-study objectives for teachers: what teachers should know about the English language and the related attitudes and skills they should have. These components represent the authors' concept of what constitutes English as a school subject. In part, they have created a Brunerian structure for this amorphous subject — a structure designed to help young people become literate and articulate.

Several fundamental principles underlie their choice, conceptualization, wording, and arrangement of objectives. First, they base these objectives upon the concept that the learning process is one of discovery, identifying the principles of learning theory and research upon which these goals are formulated — and here they are thinking of the kind of learning "that takes place in discoveries ordered by teachers who know their disciplines." Second, they have phrased most of the objectives as operational hypotheses concerning "measurable pupil performance." Third, they have classified the objectives for each component into attitudes, understandings, skills, and habits — but they do not intend to suggest by this arrangement any sequence of learning; instead, they "encourage the learner to achieve these objectives in any order and in any way that works for him." Fourth, they have ordered each list of attitudes, understandings, skills, and habits into a developmental sequence, from minimal to sophisticated objectives. And finally, as indicated above, the total list is conceived of as a way of helping each secondary-school student become "literate and articulate."

Some elements deserve special notice. Of particular importance is an emphasis that may be somewhat new to some teachers: the section on reasoning. In 1961, the Educational Policies Commission of the NEA published a report entitled *The Central Purpose of American Education.*[1] The central purpose is that of teaching American students to think. Yet many teachers of English seem not to recognize any responsibility for directly helping their students acquire and develop elements of systematic thinking, even though they have rich opportunities to help them acquire the attitudes, understandings, skills, and habits of what is called critical thinking or, in this handbook, reasoning. Professors Lazarus and Knudson provide many useful statements of what pupils ought to achieve in this aspect of their intellectual development.

[1] Washington: The National Education Association.

A second feature is the emphasis upon the development of creativeness. For the past decade or so, largely through the influence of college departments of English, teachers of English in secondary schools have emphasized expository writing, almost to the exclusion of the writing of personal essays, poetry, fiction, and drama. Now some college and university teachers of freshman English courses are giving more attention to personal writing, to the "personal voice," to the use of writers in residence in their teaching. These developments have emerged largely from an awareness that the overemphasis upon expository writing has given some teachers and students the erroneous impression that the "person" of the writer should nowhere be evident in what he writes. Professors Lazarus and Knudson have attempted to restore the balance between impersonal and personal writing by including objectives suggesting the stimulation of pupils' imaginations through their experiences with literature and with listening, speaking, and writing.

Finally, the authors emphasize throughout that learning is a process of discovery — the student's discovery. But the teacher's detailed study and testing of the hypotheses offered here, and his formulating and testing his own hypotheses, should engage him also in learning what works for him and for his students. This kind of discovery would help fulfill the authors' fourth purpose in writing this book: the stimulation of research.

This handbook should help many teachers, especially beginners, to find their way in the maze of this ill-defined subject. This is a book to be read, re-read, and referred to repeatedly by secondary-school teachers in preparing units and lesson plans and by college teachers in their instruction of future teachers. But the authors do not intend that teachers should merely transfer objectives from these pages to their daily plans as though the book were a source of "instant lessons." Such use is legitimate, but not enough. They also invite teachers to use, question, and test the statements offered here, and to write their own objectives as hypotheses to be tested. Indeed, space is provided for just this purpose. The whole point is to offer these statements not solely as a way of helping teachers to teach but also as a way of encouraging them to think of themselves as engaging in educational research, as becoming hypotheses-makers, as learning through their own discovery of what does or does not work in their own classes.

ALFRED H. GROMMON

Stanford University

Introduction

This inventory is intended to be useful to secondary-school teachers of English, to student-teachers of English and their professors, to English supervisors and leaders of in-service programs, to curriculum directors and researchers in the universities and the public schools. If we seem to be addressing students, it is only because our objectives are phrased in terms of what we expect the student to learn and do.

PURPOSES OF THE INVENTORY

Our first purpose is to select and gather into one convenient handbook certain learning objectives — some old, some new — which we have inferred from recent scholarship in literature, linguistics, and educational psychology. These learning objectives should not be misconstrued as methods of teaching; they are, rather, prerequisites for teaching methods, just as destinations are prerequisites for travel plans. However implicit methods may be here, they are far beyond the scope of this inventory.

What is needed right now, we believe, as we celebrate the explosion of knowledge in our discipline, is a concise selection from a bewildering welter of traditional, contemporary, and avant-garde objectives. Part of our selectivity consists in what we have deliberately excluded. From skills in reading literature, for example, we have excluded such current but misguided objectives as "hunting for figures of speech" and "formulating definitions of poetry," and from skills in speaking we have excluded such outmoded objectives as "holding oneself erect" and "making formal gestures" while speaking. On the other hand, we have not hesitated to include such contemporary objectives as "to understand that rules follow rather than precede or prescribe the grammar of formal speaking and writing and of informal speaking and writing . . ." and such perennially respectable objectives as "to stick to the topic" and "to respect one's audience."

We are concerned here with Grades 7–12, for in our public schools these are the grades in which English is taught as a subject, the lower grades being differently organized. Though some of our selected objectives should no doubt be acquired by pupils before they enter Grade 7, we all know that many young people in the secondary grades have yet to master them. It goes almost without saying, however, that good teaching is diagnostic; that teachers will choose from our objectives what is appropriate for given classes and individual pupils.

Our second purpose is to translate into terms of students' attitudes, understandings, skills, and habits certain learning goals championed by leaders in the field. Several of these goals are espoused by factions too ingrown to see some of the consensus that underlies their apparently irreconcilable views. The nationally visible banners of these conflicting groups proclaim "English" to be variously (1) "the tripod of literature, language, and composition," (2) "the study of oral and written communication," and (3) "experiences in reading, writing, speaking, and listening." We have rallied to the last banner in order to specify learning objectives as expectations of what the student should learn and do. To the learning-objective categories of "Reading," "Writing," "Speaking," and "Listening," we have added "Reasoning," and we have incorporated under all these "-ings" several of the goals advocated by a variety of camps. This pluralism may frustrate the monist who is convinced that his system is the only one that makes sense. But we have not been indiscriminate; our eclecticism is united by one overarching objective for young people: to become literate and articulate.

Our third purpose is to contribute to the parley, or to provoke it where none exists, between certain camps and factions. Perhaps the line is drawn most sharply between the advocates of a literature-centered and those of a language-centered curriculum. Those who accept the premise of Harold Martin, of the English Commission of the College Entrance Examination Board, that "literature is quintessentially our subject" believe that language should be learned obliquely through reading and through talking and writing about what has been read, while those who favor language as the nucleus believe that language should be learned for its own sake and as a basis for appreciating and understanding literature. Our position in this dialogue is that most of our language can and should be learned integrally with whatever is read, written, spoken, heard, and thought. We have therefore integrated into our objectives many an item which will be recognized as linguistically inspired, some under speaking, more under reading and writing. The majority of our objectives appear under reading and writing, in fact, since these are the two enterprises we believe young people need desperately to engage in above all others.

Our fourth and final purpose is to stimulate research. Thanks to such organizations as the National Council of Teachers of English (and its affiliated Conferences on Research in English, and on English Education), the Commission on English of the College Entrance Examination Board, the Modern Language Association, and the Association for Supervision and Curriculum Development, we have had many interesting delibera- tions — notably those of the Basic Issues Conferences (1959 and follow- ing) and the Anglo-American Conference at Dartmouth College (1966). What we need now is to formulate hypotheses and to test them. To be testable a hypothesis must be stated in operational terms. Part of each hypothesis (the "dependent variable") is an *objective.* This inventory includes such objectives stated in operational terms — i.e., in terms of measurable student performance.

RATIONALE OF THE "-INGS" APPROACH: THE LEARNER AS DISCOVERER

Anyone who has kept up with studies in curriculum and instruction is aware of the rebirth of interest in learning by discovery. Such pioneers in this field as Froebel, Herbart, and Dewey are now being re-examined and re-interpreted.[1] Dewey's principle of "learning by doing" was for several decades misinterpreted. The misinterpreters (inside as well as outside the profession of teaching) believed that his "doing" meant "handling things" (kinesthetics) and "going places" (field trips). Al- though Dewey did not rule out such activities — or indeed any experi- ences leading the learner to discoveries — the over-all sense of *School and Society* and of his own teaching at the Laboratory School in Chicago emphasized, rather, such "doings" as reading, writing, speaking, listening, and thinking. His pupils' activities were mostly intellectual or "mental," as he said.[2] For him, experiences in learning embraced the domains that many a contemporary behaviorist calls "cognitive" and "affective" (see, e.g., Benjamin Bloom, *et al.*, *Taxonomy of Educational Objectives, Handbook I: Cognitive Domain*[3] and its sequel, *Handbook II: Affective Domain*[4]). For Dewey, the concept of experience included thinking. If

[1] For bibliographies, see Evelyn Laurence (ed.), *Friedrich Froebel and English* [i.e., British] *Education* (New York: Philosophical Library, 1953), pp. 234–237; Lawrence Cremin, *The Transformation of the School* (New York: Alfred A. Knopf, 1962), pp. 355–387; and Richard Bernstein, *John Dewey* (New York: Washington Square Press, 1966), pp. 187–190.

[2] John Dewey, *School and Society* (Chicago: University of Chicago Press, 1899), p. 88.

[3] New York: David McKay Co., Inc., 1956.

[4] David Krathwohl, Benjamin Bloom, and Bertrand Masia, *Taxonomy of Educa- tional Objectives, Handbook II: Affective Domain* (New York: David McKay Co., 1964).

thinking ("convergent thinking" or reasoning, to say nothing of "divergent thinking" or inventing) was in his day an alien contender for any of the behavioral domains, it is much more at home in this age of computers. We now think of reasoning as a kind of selecting-rejecting performance, which computers have not yet entirely pre-empted.

Contemporary learning theorists are among the first to concede that much remains to be known about how a human being learns. But more and more of them acknowledge that the "how" depends a good deal upon the "what." B. F. Skinner, Jerome Bruner, and Lee Cronbach,[5] for example, who have otherwise disparate notions about how people learn, agree that learning takes place in discoveries ordered by teachers who know their disciplines. But it is one thing to know one's discipline — and to accept Bruner's well-known dictum that "any subject can be taught . . . in some intellectually honest form to any child at any stage of development" — and quite another thing to decide what elements ought to be taught, as Paul Woodring observes in the symposium *New Curricula*.[6] If we have presumed to decide, in our selected objectives, we are also reporting certain selections of leading scholars and schoolmen.

ORGANIZATION AND STYLE

Developmental Sequences. Having decided to list these objectives not under the various subject-matter categories ("Literature," "Language," "Rhetoric," and "Mass Media," for example) but rather under the "-ings" of student behavior, we next came to grips with the problem of what general orders these "-ings" should take. Had we been concerned with the learning of what Nelson Brooks in *Language and Language Learning* calls a "target language" (English as a second language, for instance), we could justifiably have adopted his sequence ("Listening," "Speaking," "Reading"), along with its operational hierarchy, since children first learning a language actually do listen before they speak and speak before they read. But our objectives are designed for secondary-school learners who already speak English, and who are often involved in an assortment of "ings" in any given lesson. Hence we do not imply any Brooksian sequence.

Neither do we imply the sequence "from attitude to understanding to

---

[5] Lee Cronbach, "Evaluation for Course Improvement," in *New Curricula*, ed. Robert W. Heath (New York: Harper & Row, Publishers, Inc., 1964), pp. 234–235; B. F. Skinner, "Why Teachers Fail," *Saturday Review*, 47:80–81, 98, 102; October 16, 1965. See also Marshall McLuhan, *Understanding Media* (New York: McGraw-Hill Book Co., Inc., 1964), p. vii.

[6] "Introduction" to *New Curricula*, *op. cit.*, pp. 7–8. The well-known dictum paraphrased by Mr. Woodring is from Jerome Bruner, *The Process of Education* (Cambridge, Mass.: Harvard University Press, 1960), p. 47.

skill to habit" — a sequence posited by Herbart, Morrison,[7] and others as ideal — as anything more than *one* possible and desirable working mode, in our classifications of objectives within the "ings." Although it is surely true that certain attitudes are necessary for the strengthening of certain skills and that the continual exercise of desirable skills can lead to the formation of desirable habits, it is also true that desirable attitudes are often the outcome of newly acquired understandings or skills, as B. F. Skinner and others have shown. Thus, though we have listed attitudes first, we are *not* suggesting that they *must always* precede any other achievements of learning; in fact, we encourage the learner to achieve these objectives in any order and in any way that works for him.

But the developmental sequence within each set of attitudes, understandings, skills, and habits is quite another matter, as English curriculum centers are now discovering. Each of our sets of attitudes, understandings, skills, and habits opens with minimal foundations seldom achieved, though they should be, before Grade 7 (e.g., "to comprehend the manifest and literal . . . the immediate details and circumstances [of a story or novel] . . ." and "to distinguish between simple statements of fact and simple statements of opinion"). Each set then proceeds developmentally (e.g., "to recognize 'round' and 'flat' characters" and "to detect fallacious reasoning") and ends with objectives that challenge most students, even those in the upper grades of high school (e.g., "to discover . . . symbolic levels of meaning" and "to recognize and use assumptions, definitions, hypotheses, proofs, and conclusions").

Repetition of Entries. The reader may note that there is occasional repetition and frequent near-repetition of objectives from section to section ("ings") and from subsection to subsection ("Attitudes," "Understandings," "Skills," "Habits"). This repetition is deliberate, for two reasons: (1) We assume that our readers will consult various sections and subsections of this inventory for various purposes — teachers and student teachers, for example, when they compose certain lessons in units[8] — just as they would refer to a dictionary or another kind of refer-

[7] Henry Morrison, a disciple of John Dewey's, wrote a methods book that achieved an almost Biblical status during the heyday of the Progressive Education movement in the 1930's: *The Practice of Teaching in the Secondary Schools* (Chicago: University of Chicago Press, 1931). In this book Morrison elaborately described, for the first time, what is now widely known as the unit approach. For the five developmental steps that most units reflect — preparation and presentation (cf. attitude), comparison and generalization (cf. understanding), and application (cf. skill and habit) — Morrison acknowledged his indebtedness to J. F. Herbart (1776–1841) of Königsberg. See, further, Stella Henderson, *Introduction to Philosophy of Education* (Chicago: University of Chicago Press, 1955), pp. 367–368.

[8] Like the sequence in other transactional arts, lessons in a unit are usually ordered as "initiatory," "developmental," and "culminating." These lessons begin with and are

ence work designed to be consulted here and there rather than read cover to cover. (2) By its very nature, one of our purposes in compiling this inventory — to translate into terms of students' attitudes, understandings, skills, and habits certain learning goals championed by leaders in the field (see page xx), makes unavoidable — even demands — a certain amount of repetition. Had we been interested in avoiding repetition at all costs, we could have rationalized that skills are very close to habits, or that attitudes and understandings are close enough to be combined. Similarly, we could have combined such communication arts as speaking and writing, such transaction arts as reading and listening. But we would thus only have stultified the purpose stated above, for we would have had to throw away our attempts to pin down specifications of what we believe secondary school students should achieve.

Style of Entries. For all of the entries in this handbook, we have adopted, from the traditional first sections of teachers' lesson plans, the infinitive phrase (e.g., "to value listening as civilizing and humanizing") or its extension, in which the infinitive takes as its object a nominal clause ("to realize that an accomplished listener is often regarded as a master conversationalist . . ."). Frequently, our extensions run to some length ("to make value judgments regarding a speaker's information, qualifications, intention, and presentation; to decide whether to accept or reject any part or the whole of a speech — i.e., to decide (1) whether the speaker is informed or misinformed, (2) whether the speech is logical or illogical, effectively or ineffectively presented, and (3) whether the various points made by the speaker are relevant or irrelevant, complete or incomplete"). Occasionally we call attention to undesirable responses by means of a negative objective ("to avoid listening only for facts . . ."). A negative objective cannot solo, of course; it is only the other side of its positive antithesis.

Write-Ins. A corollary of our third purpose in compiling this inventory — priming the dialogue — is to elicit from all of those who use this inventory additions, deletions, and corrections. We would be presumptuous

---

informed by objectives that range correspondingly from "attitude" to "understanding" to "skill." When there is a combination of two or more of these kinds of objectives (e.g., one attitude and two understandings), the understandings cluster in the middle and earlier lessons; the skills tend to be ordered in the culminating lessons. (Resulting habits, especially the bad ones, wait upon observations by the pupils' subsequent teachers.) When a lesson is unsuccessful the cause may go beyond trouble with objectives. But characteristically the trouble starts with the fact that the teacher has failed to settle on one or two specific objectives, so that neither he nor his pupils know where they are going or what they are supposed to accomplish. Sometimes the over-zealous teacher has elected too many objectives for one lesson — has set so many tasks for the pupil to do that no one of these tasks gets done well.

if we offered these objectives as anything more than a calculated beginning, a work in progress. And to make sure that good ideas do not evaporate, we have provided space for write-ins after each list of attitudes, understandings, skills, and habits throughout the book (see page 2, footnote 1).

TERMINOLOGY

Attitude, Understanding, Skill, Habit. By "attitude," we mean an affective response — liking or disliking. Since most of our objectives call for a favorable disposition, our attitude items begin with such infinitives as "to accept," "to respect," "to believe," "to enjoy," "to delight in," "to relish," and "to desire."

By "understanding," we intend a cognitive response. Most of these items begin with the infinitive "to understand" and "to realize." Some few begin with "to know" when whatever is to be known is more theoretical than applied.

By "skill," we mean applied understanding and knowledge — "to know how to . . ." "to be able to . . ." and "to gain competence in . . ."

By "habit," we mean the behavior pattern that results from the continual use of skills.

We intend here the kind of pattern one experiences in learning to drive a car — a pattern that (we hope) starts with appropriate attitudes and understandings (a desire to learn to be a good driver, knowledge of the strategic parts of the automobile and their functions), then progresses with enough applications of these understandings to ensure skill, and ultimately, through continual practice becomes a kind of "second nature" response.

General-Basic, Utilitarian, Expository, Imaginative. In the sections on reading and writing, the educational enterprises we believe need the most time and attention, we have sorted our entries under four subsections, "General-Basic," "Utilitarian," Expository," and "Imaginative."

By "general-basic," as the term implies, we mean the general attitudes, understandings, skills, and habits basic to reading or to writing, and common to matters dealt with in the other three subsections.

By "utilitarian," we mean the kinds of reading and writing useful in carrying on the world's work and one's livelihood — lists, notes, business letters, letters to friends, classified advertisements, minutes or proceedings of meetings, announcements, bulletins, applications and other forms to be filled in. We regard such utilitarian enterprises worthy of approximately 10 per cent of the attention that ought to be devoted to the English program as a whole.

By "expository," we mean the kinds of reading and writing sometimes thought of as (1) *investigative or informative* — news, encyclopedia articles, textbook chapters, and newspaper and magazine articles that explain "how to"; (2) *interpretive* — editorials, development-of-an-idea articles (i.e., opinion and "think-pieces"), essays in criticism, especially literary explication, and so-called essay examinations; and (3) *argumentative* — essays to convince or persuade.

Most of our expository entries deal with (2) and (3), in fact a blend of (2) and (3) — with what Sheridan Baker and others call "exposition with an argumentative edge." Leaders in the National Council of Teachers of English and in the Commission on English of the College Entrance Examination Board believe that this particular kind of exposition should no longer be the preserve of the private schools, as it has been for over one hundred years; that the public secondary schools have now come of age and are capable of benefiting from this extension to (though by no means total replacement of) their inveterate notion of "expository" as "investigative-informative." We believe that expository reading and writing deserve at least 40 per cent of the total time devoted to English in the secondary grades.

By "imaginative," we mean such genres as poetry, fiction, and drama. We believe that cultivating young people's imaginations, literary tastes, and aesthetic sensitivities deserves about 50 per cent of the total time devoted to secondary-school English. Some teachers justifiably include under "imaginative" (as do the British under "belles lettres") the familiar essay — also known as the "imaginative," "the personal" and the "informal" essay. Though the writing and reading of this genre seem to have declined, a good case could be made for their revival.

The Appendix

Our language section is an anomaly. Aside from the fact that it breaks the logic of our five "-ings" organization, it represents for the most part what we expect of teachers, not of pupils. For after we composed the objectives that the new linguistics appeared to be indicating for secondary-school students' reading, writing, and speaking, we were confronted with a number of leftovers that included some very interesting theories. These theories do not as yet seem to apply directly or completely to pupils' "-ings" and are no doubt more appropriate for study by teachers and college students (possibly also by advanced-placement and senior-elective classes in high schools).

Our conclusion about this does not clash with what certain linguists themselves have said. Many a linguist regards his discipline as an evolving science hardly ready for study by school children, though an appropriate study for teachers. What these linguists seem to be saying is that once teachers are informed in this new science (in this new "approach toward language," as Albert Marckwardt[9] has put it), they can then "reflect this orientation" in whatever classroom procedures and designs for learning they choose.

One of these ways of organizing instruction, the semester of language study for its own sake, persists amid much controversy. In addition to their claim that no language of any kind can or should be taught in isolation from literature and composition, critics of such courses charge that the language now taught in many unintegrated courses is hopelessly Latinate and prescriptive. Our choice is the integrated curriculum — in fact, the experience curriculum — but whether the teacher uses this design or some other in helping young people become literate and articulate, we believe he should know something about linguistics. We have therefore listed some of the objectives of language study in our appendix. Most of them are "Understandings," but there are a few "Attitudes."

BIBLIOGRAPHIES, SOURCES, AND ACKNOWLEDGMENTS

Besides acknowledging our indebtedness to many writers, the bibliographies following each section provide further reading for those who wish to amplify their understanding of these objectives. The bibliography for the appendix contains all of our linguistics sources, even those that have inspired some of the objectives included in the "-ings." Titles preceded by asterisks are especially recommended for beginning teachers.

Among our more general sources, only nodded to in our bibliographies, are the works of both literary scholars (Wayne Booth, David Daiches, Northrop Frye, Mark Schorer, and W. K. Wimsatt) and linguistic scholars and schoolmen (Margaret Bryant, W. Nelson Francis, Charles Fries, H. A. Gleason, Kellogg Hunt, Raven McDavid, Albert Marckwardt, Paul Roberts, Owen Thomas, and Thomas H. Wetmore). We have also drawn heavily from our own experience in public and private schools and universities and as participants and members of many conferences, committees, and commissions, particularly those of the National Council of Teachers of English, the Commission on English of the College Entrance Examination Board, and the International Reading Association.

We are deeply grateful to the following consultants for their very conscientious critical reading of our manuscript: Sam Duker, Brooklyn Col-

---

9 Quoted by Francis A. J. Ianni and Lois S. Josephs, "The Curriculum Research and Development Program of the U.S. Office of Education: Project English, Project Social Studies and Beyond," in *New Curricula, op. cit.,* p. 175. Professor Marckwardt is one of a number of the nation's linguists who have been making this important point at key conferences. For a collection of Professor Marckwardt's talks see *Linguistics and the Teaching of English* (Bloomington, Ind.: Indiana University Press, 1966).

lege; Walker Gibson, New York University; Edward J. Gordon, Yale University; Alfred Grommon, Stanford University; James B. McMillan, University of Alabama; Wayne C. Minnick, Florida State University; James Moffett, Harvard University; George Schick, Purdue University; Philip G. Smith, Indiana University; Owen Thomas, Indiana University; William Van Til, New York University; and Floyd Watkins, Emory University.

We would be remiss if we did not also acknowledge here our grateful indebtedness to the following specialists in English education, who in their speeches and conversations wittingly and unwittingly contributed one or more objectives. But they must of course be absolved from accepting or rejecting this inventory as a whole: Robert E. B. Allen, Toni Ax, Richard Alm, A. J. Beeler, Robert A. Bennett, Charles Blaney, Oscar Bouise, Sue Brett, Dwight Burton, Charles Calitri, G. Robert Carlsen, Helen Cartwright, Jeanne Chall, David Cooper, Richard Corbin, Muriel Crosby, Dorothy Davidson, Tom Devine, Wallace Douglas, Stephen Dunning, Margaret Early, Janet Emig, Verda Evans, William H. Evans, Edmund Farrell, Morris Finder, John H. Fisher, Alexander Frazier, Robert Freier, James D. Gray, Clarence Hach, Geneva Hanna, Earl Harlan, Oscar Haugh, Patrick Hazard, Louise Higgins, George Hillocks, Robert Hogan, Glenn Holder, J. N. Hook, Thomas Horn, William Hoth, Roger Hyndman, James Jarnagin, Edward Jenkinson, Arno Jewett, Lois Josephs, Stanley Kegler, Albert Kitzhaber, Barnet Kottler, Doris Kuhn, Pose Lamb, Walter Loban, Thelma McAndless, Lavinia McNeely, James Mason, Richard Meade, Joseph Murphey, Mark Neville, Paul Olson, Dorothy Petitt, Robert Pooley, Jerry Reed, Ruth Reeves, Floyd Rinker, Betty Robinett, Louise Rosenblatt, Frank Ross, Leo Ruth, Murray Satz, Bernard Schmidt, Robert E. Shafer, Michael Shugrue, John S. Simmons, Jean Sisk, Eugene Slaughter, H. Wendell Smith, George Smock, James Squire, Powell Stewart, Ingrid Strom, David Stryker, Sister Mary Sylvia, Mary Tingle, Anthony Tovatt, Lawana Trout, Donald Tuttle, Priscilla Tyler, Lizette Van Gelder, Albert Vogel, Bernard Weiss, M. Jerry Weiss, Thomas Wetmore, William Wiatt, and Grace E. Wilson.

ROZANNE KNUDSON
ARNOLD LAZARUS

Purdue University

Selected Objectives for the
English Language Arts
Grades 7-12

1

Listening

Attitudes

To enjoy listening; to take pleasure in hearing talented or skillful actors, readers, lecturers, and debaters ("live" or on television and radio and in films)

To believe that everyone's listening can be improved

To value listening as civilizing and humanizing

To regard listening as a way to learn, especially when the speaker is generally considered to be experienced and knowledgeable in a particular field or subject, yet to hold whatever one hears accountable to validation

To value group processes when members of the group are informed and competent; conversely, to be wary of the mere pooling of ignorance

To be receptive and open-minded; to be aware of the effect one's prejudices have on one's listening; to respect controversy and differences of opinion

To recognize the importance of listening (along with speaking) in democratic living; to be committed to the values of freedom of speech; to accept responsibility for thinking and evaluating while listening, regardless of whether one is given an opportunity to reply

To be tolerant toward — at times even to cherish — pronunciations and dialects different from one's own

To appreciate the pleasing sounds (and cacophonies) of the spoken word[1]

Understandings

To know why one is listening; to be aware of one's own role and motives in listening; to bring something of oneself (one's prior knowledge, for example) to listening

To be aware of the various kinds or degrees of listening: discriminating-critical, aesthetic-appreciative, informative, and escapist-relaxing

To comprehend a speaker's purpose(s) — to inform, to entertain, to convince, to persuade, to incite, to inspire

To realize that an accomplished listener is often regarded as a master conversationalist; that intelligent listening is often more rewarding than intelligent talking

[1] The space provided below, and after each subsequent set of attitudes, understandings, skills, and habits throughout the book, is for additional objectives or notes the reader may wish to write in.

Skills

To be able to follow spoken instructions

To apprehend the speaker's major point(s) and supporting points

To follow the speaker's examples and illustrations in support of his points and arguments

To follow the speaker's outline (assuming he has used one) as well as the content of his speech

To develop efficiency in taking notes while listening, avoiding attempts to take down details[2]

To make value judgments regarding a speaker's information, qualifications, intention, and presentation; to decide whether to accept or reject any part or the whole of a speech — i.e., to decide (1) whether the speaker is informed or misinformed, (2) whether the speech is logical or illogical, effectively or ineffectively presented, and (3) whether the various points made by the speaker are relevant or irrelevant, complete or incomplete

---

[2] *Note:* Though research does not suport the need for this skill, neither has research accounted as yet for the many listeners who throw their notes away and *then* perform better on recall than they do when they don't take notes at all.

To develop proficiency in selective recall; to be able to remember soon after the end of the listening experience the facts or ideas presented by the speaker that, in one's own judgment, are the most important or significant

To listen not only for the literal communication but also for what Edgar Dale calls "the mood and intent, the nuances, the mocking word, the subtly derisive allusion"[3]

To apprehend not only the words of the speaker but also his emphasis and tone of voice and (unless listening to a disembodied voice over the radio) his facial expressions

To be able to move easily from one type of listening to another — for example, from informative listening to discriminating-critical listening, from escapist-relaxing to aesthetic-appreciative

To be able to detect from a person's dialect his national or regional origin — perhaps even the city he comes from, his age, sex, educational background, and socioeconomic status

Habits

To be a listener, in conversation and discussion, as well as a speaker

---

[3] Edgar Dale, "Why Don't We Listen?" *The News Letter*, March, 1966 (Columbus, Ohio: Bureau of Educational Research, The Ohio State University), p. 1.

To listen courteously and attentively; to give the speaker an impartial hearing

To concentrate; to "tune out" whatever is irrelevant to the speaker's purpose or, in a group discussion, the purpose of the group; to ignore distractions

To rely more on one's own reactions to a speech, play, discussion, reading, or instruction from the teacher, than on those of other listeners

To look at the speaker; to try to interpret his facial expressions and other non-lingual signals

To show one's sincere feelings in listening, yet to exercise emotional control, tempering emotion with reason and open-mindedness

To listen analytically in an effort to improve one's own speech skills

To increase one's listening vocabulary day by day

To avoid such pitfalls as listening only for facts, trying to outline everything the speaker says, faking attention, and allowing emotion-laden words to interfere with listening

BIBLIOGRAPHY

Barbara, Dominick A. *The Art of Listening.* Springfield, Ill.: Charles C Thomas, Publishers, 1958.

Brown, Donald P. "Concepts and Practices in Teaching Aural English," *English Journal*, 45:540–546; December, 1956.

Brown, James I., and G. Robert Carlsen. *Brown-Carlsen Listening Comprehension Test.* New York: Harcourt, Brace & World, Inc., n.d.

Commission on the English Curriculum of the National Council of Teachers of English. *The English Language Arts in the Secondary School.* New York: Appleton-Century-Crofts, Inc., 1956. Chapter 8, "Developing Competency in Listening."

Dale, Edgar. "Why Don't We Listen?" *The News Letter*, 28, March, 1963; "Why Aren't We Smarter?" *The News Letter*, 31, March, 1966. Columbus, Ohio: Bureau of Educational Research, The Ohio State University.

*Duker, Sam. "Basics in Critical Listening," *English Journal*, 51:565–567; November, 1962.[4]

————. "Listening," *Review of Educational Research*, 34:156–163; April, 1964.

————, and C. R. Petrie, Jr. "What We Know About Listening: Continuation of a Controversy," *The Journal of Communication*, 14:245–252; December, 1964.

Edman, Irwin. "The Fairly Good Listener," *American Scholar*, 20:109–110; Winter, 1950–51.

Farrell, Edmund J. "Listen, My Children, and You Shall Read," *English Journal*, 55:39–45; January, 1966.

Frazier, Alexander, and C. E. Willson. "Learning Through Listening — to Each Other," *English Journal*, 34:367–373; September, 1950.

Gardner, John W. "The Art of Listening," *Saturday Review*, 34:45–46; June 2, 1956.

Hazard, Patrick. "Selectivity in Mass Communication," *English Journal*, 49: 646–648; December, 1960.

*Kegler, Stanley B. "Techniques in Teaching Listening for Main Ideas," *English Journal*, 45:30–32; January, 1956.

[4] Titles preceded by asterisks here and in each of the subsequent bibliographies for Sections 2, 3, 4, and 5 and the Appendix are especially recommended for beginning teachers.

*McKinney, Eleanor (ed.). *The Exacting Ear*. New York: Pantheon Books, 1966.

*McLuhan, Marshall. *Understanding Media*. New York: McGraw-Hill Book Co., Inc., 1964.

Mannes, Marya. "Who Owns the Air?" (leaflet). Milwaukee, Wisc.: Marquette University Press, 1959.

Minow, Newton. "And Now, a Message to the Sponsor" (a DuPont Awards Foundation leaflet). Lexington, Va.: Washington and Lee University, 1964.

Nichols, Ralph G. "Listening Instruction in the Secondary School," in *Teaching English in Today's High Schools*, ed. Dwight L. Burton and John S. Simmons. New York: Holt, Rinehart & Winston, Inc., 1965.

*————. "Listening Is a Ten-Part Skill," *Nation's Business*, 45:56–60; July, 1957.

————, and Leonard A. Stevens. *Are You Listening?* New York: McGraw-Hill Book Co., Inc., 1957.

*Russell, David H., and Elizabeth F. Russell. *Listening Aids Through the Grades — One-Hundred-Ninety Listening Activities*. New York: Bureau of Publication, Teachers College, Columbia University, 1959.

Schreiber, Morris. *An Annotated List of Recordings in the Language Arts*. Champaign, Ill.: The National Council of Teachers of English, 1964.

Sequential Tests of Educational Progress: Listening. Princeton, N.J.: Educational Testing Service, 1957.

Whyte, William H. *Is Anybody Listening?* New York: Simon and Schuster, Inc., 1952.

Witty, Paul (ed.). *Studies in Listening*. Champaign, Ill.: The National Council of Teachers of English, 1959.

2

....

Speaking

Attitudes

To enjoy speaking

To believe that everyone's speaking can be improved

To value (but not over-value) one's speaking experiences as a means of self-expression and self-fulfillment

To respect one's audience; to try to interest or entertain (depending upon one's purpose in speaking), as well as to instruct or persuade

To appreciate and admire articulate speaking

To prefer the use of clear, accurate, and compelling language in one's speech; to prefer fresh, lively language over the cliché

To recognize the importance of speech in democratic living; to cherish freedom of speech

To cultivate an attitude of responsibility for speaking honestly and for shunning mere rhetoric

To be willing to discuss a wide range of topics, from the commonplace to the controversial

To respect simplicity and clarity of expression; to value the understanding of an ability to use complex words and phrases or expressions borrowed from foreign languages, but to use them only when they seem more appropriate or more expressive than the simpler words and phrases or the more familiar native ones

Understandings

To understand that communicating (writing as well as speaking) is a three-stage transaction involving (1) sender, (2) message, and (3) receiver; that the more careful attention one gives to all three of these stages, the better are one's chances for successful communication

To understand the purpose and scope of a discussion; to be aware of the topics and techniques of good discussion; to understand that as a general rule one of the least interesting topics of discussion is one which the speaker regards as absolute or incontrovertible; one of the more interesting, whatever the speaker regards as open to speculation

To realize that although one should strive to learn "new" words and use them in speaking, one's speaking vocabulary should be simpler than one's writing vocabulary and certainly not as sophisticated as one's reading vocabulary

To know the chief characteristics of effective speech: that speech begins with thought; that it is ideally social and purposeful; and that it requires an appropriate attitude toward one's listeners (e.g., the type of audience one is addressing may justify or fail to justify the use of jargon or slang)

To know when to be animated and when to be restrained, according to one's purpose

To understand that whenever a speaker in literature or life makes an utterance, he almost always reveals one or more of the following: his historical era, his geographical origin (country, region, locality), his age group (infancy, childhood, adolescence, adulthood, old age), his sex, the age and sex of his audience, the size of his audience (from intimate to public), his formal education (or lack of it), his socioeconomic status, his values, sports, and pastimes

To understand that much of our contemporary slang began as a kind of argot in such vocations as trucking, jazz-playing, and the armed services;[1] that slang is an extremely informal kind of speech, if not as volatile as it was once thought to be; and that it is not appropriate in formal communication

To understand that there is no such thing as "absolutely correct" or "absolutely incorrect" usage; that various "standard," "nonstandard," and "substandard" classifications are based on regional and occasional levels of acceptability or prestige; that the terms "formal," "informal" (or "colloquial"), and "slang" are not levels but rather *functional varieties of usage;*[2] that further refining of these functional varieties produces what Martin Joos and others have called the "continua" and "clocks of usage"[3] (for example, at various times and in various situations or "functions" one may speak *formally* to a large or unfamiliar audience, then later *informally*, or casually or even intimately, to a single friend or relative)

To realize that usage is relative; that "correctness" or appropriateness depends upon the dimensions of time, place, occasion, and audience, as Robert Pooley has put it in *Teaching English Usage:*

[1] See H. L. Mencken and Raven McDavid, *The American Language* (New York: Alfred A. Knopf, Inc., 1963), Chapter 11, "American Slang."

[2] See J. S. Kenyon, "Cultural Levels and Functional Varieties," in *Readings in Applied English Linguistics*, 2nd ed., ed. Harold B. Allen (New York: Appleton-Century-Crofts, Inc., 1964); Margaret M. Bryant, *Current American Usage* (New York: Funk and Wagnalls Company, 1962); and P. B. Gove, "Status Labels," in "Explanatory Notes," *Webster's Seventh New Collegiate Dictionary* (Springfield, Mass.: G. & C. Merriam Co., Publishers, 1965), p. 11a.

[3] Martin Joos, *The Five Clocks* (Bloomington, Ind.: Indiana University Press, 1962).

Good English usage is that form of speech which is appropriate to the purpose of the speaker, true to the language as it is, and comfortable to speaker and listener. It is the product of custom, neither cramped by rule nor freed from all restraint . . .[4]

To understand that rules follow rather than precede or prescribe the grammar of formal speaking and writing and of informal speaking and writing; that most educated, well-read people say, for example, "Who is this for?" and "Which school did you go to?" (instead of "For whom is this?" and "To which school did you go?")

To understand that meanings are signaled partly by intonational clues, by stress and pause (e.g., the utterance, "This is a silent movie house," can have at least two different meanings according to whether there is a pause between "silent" and "movie house" or between "silent movie" and "house")

To understand that an effective formal speech reflects planning, and that this planning includes an analysis of the intended audience, occasion, and purpose, along with the careful selection of points to be made, examples and data to be used for illustration, and careful organizing

To understand the roles of the chairman or moderator and of the participants in symposia and panel discussions

To become familiar with the basic, most widely practiced rules of parliamentary procedure

To understand how to present an interesting and informative oral book review — for example, by reading a brief, significant passage (previously selected), then explaining its meaning in light of the book's main theme or issues; to know why certain unacceptable practices should be avoided — among them, rehashing the plot of a novel

[4] (New York: Appleton-Century-Crofts, Inc., 1946), p. 14.

Skills

To have memorized (preferably before Grade 7) the principal parts of verbs frequently confused, such as "sit," "sat," "sat"; "fly," "flew," "flown"; "flow," "flowed," "flowed," as one of the bases toward establishing competence and confidence in speaking

To have developed (preferably before Grade 7) a pleasant, flexible, and clearly audible voice

To master (preferably before Grade 7) such social skills as introducing people to each other, telephoning, and giving geographical directions

To be competent in using the language idiomatically in speaking as well as in writing

To be able to read orally with intelligent interpretation and expression; to be able to read fluently with appropriate rhythm

To develop the ability to make announcements before a group

To induce speaking skills from hearing and observing speakers

To develop poise in public speaking; to develop the ability to express one's thoughts and feelings with ease before a group

To stick to the topic (except possibly in speeches intended to entertain)

To make a straightforward, sincere presentation — except when one's purpose is deliberately not to inform, convince, persuade, or inspire (i.e., when one's purpose is to entertain or amuse)

To learn to use unobtrusive gestures, which reflect confidence, sincerity, and self-control

To adjust the volume of one's voice to acoustical conditions; to vary pitch and rate of speaking for purposes of emphasis; to phrase and pause effectively

To choose diction appropriate to audience, occasion, and purpose; to use informal language for such informal occasions as talks before small groups; to use formal language for such formal functions as debates, symposia, salutatory addresses, and "platform introducing" of outside guests to school audiences

To have a ready supply of synonyms and antonyms for use in speaking; in homework, in classwork, and in preparation for giving a talk before an audience, to be able to find synonyms or antonyms efficiently in a dictionary or thesaurus; to be able to discriminate among synonyms

To be able to achieve rapport with one's listeners; to start, for example, with statements that most of them will probably accept before building up to the more controversial opinions or arguments

To develop the ability to ask pertinent questions as well as to answer them

To be able to explain clearly and sufficiently; to use examples, when possible, to clarify meanings

To master the art of carrying on intelligent, interesting, and courteous discussions and conversations; to develop a pleasant but unaffected tone of voice

To cultivate articulateness in speaking extemporaneously in panel and group discussions

To develop the ability to lead a discussion as well as to participate in one

To be able to select discussion problems suitable to the age, maturity, and interests of the discussants

To cultivate the ability to convince and persuade

To be able to dramatize passages of dialogue in fiction or plays; to "get into the skins" of the characters

To develop skill in debating; e.g., (1) to keep tone of voice and gestures restrained, avoiding histrionics; (2) to anticipate and demolish opponents' arguments; (3) during the rebuttal, to be honest, if devastating, and to avoid misrepresenting opponents' arguments

Habits

To speak clearly — to enunciate

To show more interest, in conversation, in the person spoken to than in oneself

To take an active, co-operative part in discussions; to respond as well as to listen

To use every opportunity for speech improvement; to express ideas clearly and purposefully

To consider the needs and desires of one's audience — for example, to be interested, to be informed, to be stimulated to think, to be entertained — and speak accordingly

To persuade, when expressing a controversial point of view, by presenting evidence and by using reason rather than emotion

To maintain eye contact with one's audience; to utilize "feedback" by observing the listeners with respect and understanding

To avoid being an offensive speaker, one who monopolizes conversations or discussions, one who interrupts constantly, who "shouts down" other speakers, who talks for display rather than communication

To increase one's speaking vocabulary day by day

To gain increasing sensitivity, through continual use, to the most appropriate language for each occasion of speaking (and writing)[5]

BIBLIOGRAPHY

Andersch, Elizabeth, and Lorin Staats. *Speech for Everyday Use.* New York: Holt, Rinehart & Winston, Inc., 1962.

Barnes, Grace, and Mary Jean Sutcliffe. *On Stage, Everyone.* New York: The Macmillan Co., 1964.

Bernstein, Abraham. *Teaching English in High School.* New York: Random House, Inc., 1961. Chapter 10, "Speech."

Cherry, Colin. *On Human Communication.* Cambridge, Mass.: Technology Press of The Massachusetts Institute of Technology, 1957.

Early, Margaret J. "Communication Arts," in *Encyclopedia of Educational Research,* ed. Chester W. Harris. New York: The Macmillan Co., 1960.

Fowler, Mary Elizabeth. *Teaching Language, Composition, and Literature.* New York: McGraw-Hill Book Co., Inc., 1965. Chapter 4, "Speaking and Listening: A Two-Way Process."

*Frazier, Alexander. "Making the Most of Speaking-and-Listening Experiences," in *Teaching English in Today's High Schools,* ed. Dwight L. Burton and John S. Simmons. New York: Holt, Rinehart & Winston, Inc., 1965.

---

[5] See the "Usage Glossary" in Louis Zahner, Arthur Mullin, and Arnold Lazarus, *The English Language, Senior Course* (New York: Harcourt, Brace & World, Inc., 1966), especially pp. 428–429.

*Hedde, Wilhelmina G., William N. Brigance, and Victor Powell. *The New American Speech*. Philadelphia: J. B. Lippincott Co., 1963.

Jenkinson, Edward, *et al.* (eds.). *Teacher's Guide to High School Speech*. Indianapolis: Indiana State Department of Public Instruction, 1966.

Loban, Walter, Margaret Ryan, and James R. Squire. *Teaching Language and Literature*. New York: Harcourt, Brace & World, Inc., 1961. Chapter 9, "Oral Language."

McBath, James (ed.). *Argumentation and Debate*. New York: Holt, Rinehart & Winston, Inc., 1954.

Mersand, Joseph, *et al. Guide to Play Selection*. New York: Appleton-Century-Crofts, Inc., 1958.

Monroe, Alan H., and Douglas Ehninger. *Principles of Speech* (5th brief ed.) Chicago: Scott, Foresman & Company, 1964.

Robert, Henry Martyn. *Rules for Order*. Chicago: Scott, Foresman & Company, 1951.

Sarett, Alma, Lew Sarett, and W. T. Foster. *Basic Principles of Speech* (4th ed.). Boston: Houghton Mifflin Company, 1966.

*Thompson, David W., and Virginia Fredericks. *Oral Interpretation of Fiction: A Dramatistic Approach*. Minneapolis: Burgess Publishing Company, 1964.

*Wagner, Russell, and Carroll Arnold. *Handbook of Group Discussion* (2nd ed.). Boston: Houghton Mifflin Company, 1965.

Wolfe, Don M. *Creative Ways to Teach English* (2nd ed.). New York: The Odyssey Press, 1966. Chapter 8, "Speech Resources in the Democratic Classroom."

3
....

Reading

A. GENERAL-BASIC

Attitudes

To enjoy reading

To believe that everyone's reading can be improved

To be committed to reading as a lifetime experience and to Francis Bacon's observation that "Reading maketh a full man"

To enjoy library visits; to cherish the library as a civilizing institution

To desire the knowledge, insight, and aesthetic appreciation that one can get from reading many different kinds of books and periodicals

To appreciate the talent and skill of professional writers; to savor, in one's reading, the surprisingly apt expression

To prefer, more often than not, serious reading to "entertainments"; yet to accept one's need for an occasional change of pace (to be willing to read detective stories, for example, or "light" novels or verse)

17

To recognize the importance of reading in democratic living; to value reading as a way of becoming better informed and thus better able to participate more intelligently in democratic institutions

Understandings

To realize that there are several kinds of reading — among them, browsing, skim reading, and analytic reading

To understand that one reads for many purposes; to know one's purpose for reading a given piece

To understand that different kinds of reading require different reading rates

To understand that once one has decreased his eye-fixations and regressions, has increased his efficiency in word-recognition and in reading by phrases, he is then only at the threshold of the skills in depth reading specified below (in the sections on reading exposition and imaginative literature)

To realize that reading improves with reading and with instruction in reading

To realize that one's recognition or reading vocabulary needs to be much larger than one's writing and speaking vocabularies

To realize that dictionary meanings may not fit a word's use in context; that a dictionary is essentially a report on how people use particular utterances in characteristic situations; that no dictionary is large enough (not even the many-volumed *Oxford Dictionary*) to report on uses of a word or expression in uncharacteristic situations

To understand that authors almost always imply more than they say in so many words; to understand that reading is a transaction the reader makes with the writer, as Louise Rosenblatt has pointed out[1]

To understand that authors "ride on the backs of other authors"; that they refer and allude to their predecessors; that literature is a heritage as well as a stimulus for inventive departure[2]

To be aware of the fact that there is a wide range of excellence (and lack of excellence) in reading materials; that just as we become physically what we ingest and digest, so we shape our intellectual and aesthetic tastes in large part by what we read

Skills

To become competent (preferably before Grade 7) in using appropriate phonemic stresses (e.g., "cóntent" or "contént" according to context) and appropriate configurational stress (e.g., "wherever you *go*") in silent as well as in oral reading; in short, to read by word groups rather than word by word

[1] Louise Rosenblatt, "The Acid Test for Literature Teaching," *English Journal*, 45:66–74; February, 1956.
[2] See John Livingston Lowes, *Convention and Revolt in Poetry* (Boston: Houghton Mifflin Company, 1919), and T. S. Eliot, *The Sacred Wood* (New York: Alfred A. Knopf, 1921), "Tradition and the Individual Talent," p. 42 ff.

To improve such motor skills as widening of eye-span, increasing the length of rhythmic eye-stops, and reducing regressions to zero

To increase speed in reading while maintaining comprehension; to be able to "shift gears" in reading — to adjust speed of reading to what is being read

To recognize syntactic and typographical cues; for example, to note the meaning signaled by the words "such . . . as" in the sentence: "Such writers as Corbiere, La Forgue, and Valery inspired T. S. Eliot"; to note the meaning signaled by capital letters, parentheses, and boldface and italic type

To know and be able to use classical prefixes, roots, and suffixes in words obviously built upon them, as clues to derivative meanings, but to be on guard against etymological fallacies — e.g., the word "education" is not derived from "educere" ("to lead out") but rather from "educare" ("to nourish") — even if its primitive meaning has gone out of fashion

To be able to apprehend the significance of a work's title; to note whether it suggests more than it says and whether it is a comment on the work

To determine the writer's purpose (e.g., to inform, to persuade, to entertain) implicit in the genre (biography, petition, play) and in the mode (satire, romance, comedy, tragedy)[3]

To recognize main ideas, supporting details, sequences of events, and causal relationships; to draw appropriate conclusions; to make inferences; to predict outcomes

To be able to distinguish between denotation and connotation

---

[3] *Note:* Trying to determine purpose other than that which is manifest in the genre or mode of a work may result in what W. K. Wimsatt calls "intentional fallacy."

Habits

To gain increasing acquaintance with good books and reputable authors; to continually read a wide range of books and periodicals — fiction and non-fiction, classic and modern, and on a variety of subjects[4]

To keep a log of one's opinions about what one has read

To extend and enrich one's vocabulary through extensive and intensive reading

To keep an individual notebook of "Newly-Learned Words" with contextual excerpts as well as definitions, even if such a notebook is thrown away once one has this vocabulary in one's head

To read with a pencil; to cultivate the habit of annotating one's own (not the school's or the library's) books, by underscoring what seem to be the important and perhaps memorable passages and by adding in the margins identifying "tags," "cf.'s," cross-references, and one's own critical reactions[5]

To develop a sense of humor; to look for affectations and incongruities in characters; to look for irony and "pleasant disappointments of expectation" in prose and verse, direct and indirect discourse

To cultivate intellectual curiosity; to continually consult not only dictionaries (for vocabulary and allusions) but also critical books and essays; yet to prefer primary to secondary sources — i.e., to prefer reading a great novel to reading an essay about it

[4] See Committee on College Reading of the College English Association, *Good Reading*, ed. J. Sherwood Weber (New York: Mentor Books, 1960), and Committee on the Senior High School Book List of the National Council of Teachers of English, *Books for You* (New York: Washington Square Press, Inc., 1964).

[5] See Mortimer Adler, "How to Mark a Book," in *Adventures in Modern Literature*, ed. Robert Freier and Arnold Lazarus (New York: Harcourt, Brace & World, Inc., 1962), pp. 517–521.

To build one's own library, now that good books are available in inexpensive editions

B. UTILITARIAN

Attitudes

To accept the fact that, although utilitarian reading and research may not be as interesting or challenging as some other kinds of reading, it is necessary, and it need not always be dull

To be curious; to say, in effect, "I want to know" and "I want to find out"; to derive satisfaction from searching for and finding information

To prefer, in general, facts to speculation; to want to know and recognize the distinguishing characteristics of factual writing

Understandings

To understand that the first and quickest way to locate information in an encyclopedia is by using the index rather than the alphabetical volume-listings, since many entries are not included under these alphabetical listings but under some other, often unanticipated, listing

To know the parts of the newspaper and their functions and purposes

To know the general classifications of magazines; to know the kinds of articles (for reference purposes) published by such magazines as *The Nation,* the *New Republic,* the *Saturday Review, Harper's,* the *Atlantic Monthly,* and others

Skills

To be able to follow written directions; to interpret accurately what is asked for in applications and examinations

To be able to use tables of contents, indexes, and headings and other typographical cues as aids in reading

To be able to use library tools, such as the card catalogue and *Readers' Guide to Periodical Literature* efficiently; to develop facility in locating information in the library

To develop competence in using the dictionary to find definitions and spellings, determine pronunciations, learn derivations, recognize various shades of meaning and interpret each observation made about a word

To know how to use the standard sources and tools of the researcher: dictionaries such as *Webster's Third New International Dictionary Unabridged, Webster's New Collegiate, Funk and Wagnall's Standard, Webster's New World, The Random House Dictionary of the English Language,* and the *American College Dictionary;* encyclopedias such as the *Britannica* and the *Americana;* publishers' trade lists; almanacs; *Who's Who, Current Biography;* and other reference books

To be able to summarize passages succinctly; to be able to make oral or written précis of what one has read or to outline what one has read

Habits

To make constant use of libraries

To read regularly two or three well-known newspapers and magazines in order to be informed of national and international developments, current issues and arguments, and to know where to locate these issues in reasonably reliable form

To keep one's own bibliography of available sources for various kinds of information

C. EXPOSITORY

Attitudes

To enjoy reading controversial opinions and trying to distinguish between opinions and facts

To be committed to the discovery of truth, insofar as it can be discovered

To respect the right of authors to express opinions different from one's own

Understandings

To realize that most of what is published today is non-fiction, or is so intended

To understand the demands and purposes of expository writing (to inform, to explain, to interpret, to explicate, to illuminate, to defend, to attack, to convince)

To be familiar with major periods, movements, and trends in literary history but to avoid overemphasizing the importance of this information at the expense of acquaintance with the major literary works themselves

To understand that much of what is called "fact" is permeated with opinion — i.e., that writers are always selective in collecting, judging, and presenting information, that they abstract from factual documents only certain portions for reconstructing expository accounts and essays, and that sometimes an author distorts the truth either through ignorance or deliberately, for a certain effect

To realize that biographers ordinarily choose not to reveal everything they know about living subjects; that often discretion rules what will be told the general public, at least until after the subject's death

Skills

To develop such skills in critical reading as (1) postponing evaluation until one has thoroughly understood what the author has said, meant, assumed, and implied; (2) evaluating whether the author's writing is informed or misinformed, complete or incomplete, logical or illogical, relevant or irrelevant; (3) deciding how much one can or cannot accept and why, and recognizing which examples are and which are not in support of the thesis; (4) evaluating to what degree the author is successful in what he says and the way he says it

To recognize how the parts of an essay or article or chapter of a book fit within the whole; conversely, to be able to analyze the whole into its parts; to recognize relationships between details and main ideas

To be able to distinguish fact from opinion insofar as this is possible

To be able to find an author's thesis statement

To follow the author's line of argument and support for a thesis

To be able to restate main points accurately

To apprehend emphases, not just by such typographical and punctuational cues as italics and exclamation points, but also (and especially) by the amount of space allotted to certain points and arguments in relation to the whole

To recognize meanings of key terms in context — what Mortimer Adler calls "coming to terms"[6] — and whether the author ever does define his key terms, either explicitly, or implicitly through the context

To be able to read for key words, transitions, and specific details

To be able to distinguish between non-emotional and emotional (loaded) language

To recognize implications; to discern assumptions; to draw inferences

To recognize the author's attitude or bias toward his material

To recognize conventions of content and structure of a newspaper "story"; of a feature article

To recognize conventions of content and structure of a magazine article; to distinguish informative from argumentative articles; to grasp the thesis of an essay with an argumentative edge

To distinguish between biographies and memoirs; between types of biography and autobiography such as the *official*, the *romantic*, and the *socio-historical*

To know (or know where to find) the sources of materials for biographies

[6] *How to Read a Book* (New York: Simon and Schuster, Inc., 1940), Chapter 2, ff.

and autobiographies (letters, diaries, journals, and memoirs); for a biography, to be able to state the author's point of view and his method (narrative, psychological-introspective) of developing it

Habits

To read *critically* only after one has read *structurally* (comprehension of whole to parts; parts to whole) and *interpretively* (discovering connotations); to work toward a more and more automatic blending of these skills[7]

To develop a critical spirit; that is, to be constantly alert to conflicting ideas or points of view, to the difference between denotation and connotation, between fact and opinion, between emotional and non-emotional language

To look for and compare differences of opinion in editorials and articles

To recognize accurate and thorough coverage of facts in various kinds of expository articles and essays; to distinguish fact from opinion or speculation, insofar as this is possible

To become increasingly familiar with such publications as *Atlantic* and *Harper's; The Nation, New Republic,* and *The Reporter;* the *Saturday Review,* the *New York Review of Books;* and others

[7] *Ibid.* Chap. 7, p. 124.

D. IMAGINATIVE

Attitudes

To enjoy reading literature of all kinds — contemporary and classic, sophisticated works of art and homely folklore

To value reading as humanizing and civilizing

To desire the understanding of life in its personal, social, and aesthetic phases that one can gain from literature

To regard literature as "the best that has been thought and said" — i.e., as good *writing;* (conversely, to regard good writing as potential literature — i.e., as having a chance for permanence)

To be interested in acquiring familiarity with literature from beyond the shores of England and the United States

To accept the fact that a continuum of quality exists in literature; that one doesn't always need the "test of time" to discriminate

To cultivate aesthetic sensitivities, among them a love of the sensuous and an appreciation of the imaginative recreation of human experience

To resist Puritanical, anti-aesthetic attitudes; to rejoice that more and more American communities are accepting and encouraging the arts

Understandings

To understand that literature is one of the arts; that it is a re-creation in words (comparable to re-creations in paint, stone, and sound) of what it is like to be alive

To understand the principle of *aesthetic distance* — i.e., that once a literary work has been created, it goes forth on its own as a new entity with an integrity of its own; that therefore the reader should guard against jumping to erroneous conclusions regarding relationships between the author's life and elements in the literary work

To understand that every major work of literature (like any other work of art) has a logic of its own, a certain integrity in which its form and content are just right for each other; that its theme is treated in a special way, even if it is a theme that is common to many other literary works

To be familiar with some of the major themes in literature — among them, the search for self, love for another person, love of country, heroism, the search for wisdom, personal integrity, alienation, the individual and society, crime and punishment, war and peace, and others

To understand that (just as *form* signals *meaning* in an utterance) the *genre* of a literary work (i.e., whether it is a short story, novel, play, or poem) contributes part of the meaning

To understand relationships between life and literature; to understand that literature, like the fine arts, selects from rather than photographs life; that the observation "this is lifelike" is not as much a compliment to an author as is the observation "life is like this"

To gain an awareness, in reading literature, of human aspirations shared in common, of the clash of values, of the significance of everyday experience

To know major authors, forms, movements; yet to understand that the reading of chronological surveys cannot be as rewarding as reading some major authors in depth

To recognize that no country or part of the world has a monopoly on literature; that quite often English and American literature is indebted, in one way or another, to Continental, Near Eastern, and Far Eastern literature

To understand that the world created in any literary work may *reflect* the real world but is essentially a world of its own

To understand that there is often more than one interpretation of a literary work; that "pluralism" is not chaos; that a number of interpretations can often be supported by the details of a given work

To understand the distinguishing characteristics of such genres as poems, plays, stories, novels, fables, parables, and allegories

To understand that for each genre, despite variations on it, in particular literary pieces, there are certain traditional conventions (e.g., a well-known convention of the fairy tale is that it begins "Once upon a time . . ." and ends ". . . and they lived happily ever after"; a convention of certain Italianate sonnets is that the first eight lines present a problem which is resolved in the last six lines)

To understand that the meaning of a literary work is partly signaled by its tone, texture, and context

To understand the author's *tone*, his attitude toward his material; it is of course this attitude (ironical, serious, humorous, whimsical) which informs the mode and meaning of a piece

To understand the concept of modes — that meaning is signaled by (and is almost impossible to apprehend without knowledge of) the fact that a given literary work is comedy, tragedy, tragi-comedy, romance, satire, or parody[8]

To understand that many a poem, play, or story has at its center irony, or paradox, or some artistically developed contrast (light and shade, or *chiaroscuro*)

To understand the work's cultural context or ethos (mores and pastimes), perhaps the more challenging aspects of setting, which certainly need more study than do the manifest "what" and "where" of the setting

To understand character *foils* in fiction, drama, and epic poetry; to understand contrastive traits of character (e.g., of Ulysses and Telemachus, Falstaff and Hal, Billy Budd and Claggart)

To understand some of the distinctions between humor and wit, among them the fact that humor arises out of character and situation whereas wit arises out of brilliant irreverence; to understand that both humor and wit are pleasant disappointments of expectation

To understand the chief distinctions between satire and parody, i.e., that satire ridicules human institutions and weaknesses — vices, folly, abuses, or shortcomings — while parody mimics a writer's language and style, contains less sting, and can even be a compliment to the victim[9]

To understand symbolism[10]

To understand some of the relationships between genres: that some novels contain philosophical essays; that novels and plays share in common certain kinds of scenes and summaries — in fact, that a narrative often summarizes several little dramas; that drama embeds a good deal of narrative summation in the lines spoken by the actors, especially in poetic Greek drama, in which the narrative is summarized by the chorus

To understand some of the relationships between genres and basic utterance patterns; to understand, e.g., that plays, stories, and narrative

---

[8] Northrop Frye, *Anatomy of Criticism* (Princeton, N. J.: Princeton University Press, 1957).

[9] See Gilbert Highet, *The Anatomy of Satire* (Princeton, N.J.: Princeton University Press, 1962), "Satire and Truth," pp. 148–159, and "Types of Literary Parody," pp. 103–147.

[10] See Edmund Wilson, *Axel's Castle* (New York: Charles Scribner's Sons, 1931), Chapter 1, "Symbolism."

poems echo the S/V/O or S/V/iO/O sentence patterns, in which someone does something or does someone good or evil; that essays and lyric
poems echo the S/LV/C[11] pattern, in which "x is y" (metaphor and
symbolism)[12]

Skills

To apprehend the literal and the manifest as an indispensable beginning;
to avoid attempting "depth reading" until after one has first appre-
hended what is on the surface

To relate form and content, and to recognize how very often the two are
inextricable

To recognize an author's virtuosity with language — especially his precision with denotative and with connotative expressions

To discover possibilities of meaning in metaphor, allegory, symbolism,
and myth

To avoid trying to explicate by general, unqualified rules, which are bound
to betray if not disappoint, e.g., to expect conventional plot structure
in the "anti-play" of the theater of the absurd (see, further, D–3,
"Drama," page 46)

To recognize *paradox* (apparent inconsistency); to distinguish it from

---

[11] Subject / Linking Verb / Complement.
[12] See, further, Kenneth Burke, *A Grammar of Motives* (New York: Prentice-Hall,
Inc., 1954), "Introduction," pp. xxvi, and *The Philosophy of Literary Form* (New
York: Vintage Books, 1961), "Ritual Drama as Hub," pp. 87–113.

irony (intentional disappointment of expectation) and from *dramatic irony* (irony that not all the characters are aware of)

To recognize ethical values in literature and to discuss them with others

To be able to compare one piece of literature to another with respect to genre, mode, theme, texture, and style

To recognize references and allusions to mythologies, folklore, the Bible; to Homer, Virgil, Dante, Chaucer, Shakespeare, and many other celebrated writers, ancient and modern

To recognize parody[13]

To recognize archetypal experiences and characters, among them the journey of the hero, the decline and fall of the powerful, the adventurer's wheel of fortune, the alienation of the outsider, the ordeal of the initiate and of the scapegoat

Habits

To develop the imagination through the reading of literature

To develop sensitivity to beauty and to human feelings through literature

To read in depth at least one author, one genre, one period

[13] See, e.g., Dwight Macdonald, *Parodies: An Anthology from Chaucer to Beerbohm — and After* (New York: Random House, Inc., 1960).

To extend continually one's acquaintance with our literary heritage through reading; to avoid trying to build such an acquaintance through reading literary history alone

To memorize certain well-known (and even some not-so-well-known) passages from poetry, drama, and fiction

To seek, from one's reading, insights into human experience, awareness of the complexity of human character and of oneself in relation to other people; to receive reinforcement for one's attitudes and convictions and to develop new ones; to make reading a kind of transaction between author and reader

To form an opinion of or to make a judgment of a literary work only after one has carefully read the work and interpreted it; to prefer internal evidence ("the primary text") to external evidence or what someone else may have said about it ("secondary sources")

To develop critical attitudes toward ethical values, toward qualities of excellence and of depravity in characters of fiction, drama, and poetry

To relate literature to other art forms

To develop increasingly more sophisticated tastes in reading

To delight in recognizing rhetorical devices but to avoid hunting and labeling them (See James Thurber's "Here Lies Miss Groby," *The Thurber Carnival*)

1. Poetry

Attitudes

To respect poetry as a priceless art form, as something that may heighten one's sensitivity to living

To accept the fact that poetry is essentially secular and hedonistic — that it celebrates things of this world, as John Crowe Ransom and others have observed

To regard as possible treasures the poems one likes now, but to be willing to reassess this treasury, from time to time, subjecting it to one's changing tastes

To appreciate the beauty of sound in poetry, and the relationship between sound and sense

To enjoy discovering the paradoxes and planned ambiguities of poems[14]

Understandings

To understand what is said literally, in a poem, but also to understand that what happens on the surface is only a beginning to discovering

---

[14] See William Empson, *Seven Types of Ambiguity* (New York: Meridian Books, 1957); also, May Swenson, "A Clue or Two" [preface of] *Poems to Solve* (New York: Charles Scribner's Sons, 1966).

possibilities of meanings beneath the surface; that within a poem there is often more than one layer of meaning, aside from the intentional ambiguities in individual words

To understand imagery and the image-metaphor-symbol complex; to understand how images (any concrete appeals to any of the senses) are the basic building-blocks of metaphor and symbol[15]

To understand the concept of "objective correlatives"; to understand that master poets tend to understate, to prefer using carefully selected objective images and experiences which correlate not only with the theme of the poem but also with the experience or imagination of the reader in order to re-create in him the kinds of emotions experienced by the poet[16]

To understand rhythm and meter: the chief meters and stanza forms

To understand the characteristics of free verse — for example, freedom from the very limited repertoire of rimes available in English and from the "padding" that rime often imposes

To understand that "you can spot the bad critic when he starts by discussing the poet and not the poem."[17]

To understand that almost every poem has a logic of its own; that generalities and rules are likely to betray the explicator; that many a poem is in part like a unique puzzle to be solved on its own terms

To understand that in an utterance like "Ulysses sailed the wine-dark sea" the modifier "wine-dark" probably represents a reduction of an S/LV/C[18] sentence pattern such as "the sea was wine-dark"; that much of the dense texture (what Owen Thomas[19] and others call "transformational density") of poetry, especially of poems like those of Emily Dickinson, is the result of embedding into one or another of the basic simple-sentence patterns ("kernels") a modifier reduced from what was

---

[15] See William Butler Yeats, "The Symbolism of Poetry," in *Literary Symbolism,* ed. Maurice Beebe (Belmont, Calif.: Wadsworth Publishing Company, 1960).

[16] "Objective correlative" is closely related to Keats' concept of "negative capability." See Lionel Trilling (ed.), *The Selected Letters of John Keats* (New York: Farrar, Straus & Young, 1951), p. 92.

[17] Ezra Pound, *A B C of Reading* (New York: New Directions Press, 1960), p. 84.

[18] Subject / Linking Verb / Complement.

[19] See Owen Thomas, *Transformational Grammar and the Teacher of English* (New York: Holt, Rinehart & Winston, Inc., 1965), Chapter 8.

originally, in prose, another sentence; for example, in the poem "Bring me the Sunset in a Cup" the utterance "the new robin's ecstasy" compresses such S/LV/C kernels as "the robin is new," "the robin is ecstatic," "the robin's song is ecstatic," and even "the newness is ecstatic"

Skills

To be able to read poetry (preferably before Grade 7) without a singsong drop of voice indiscriminately at the end of each line; to be able to follow through from line to line ("enjambement") except when punctuation signals a stop

To apply, in reading poetry, one's knowledge of sentence patterns — especially of S/V, S/V/O, and S/LV/C patterns; to be able to locate in a poem, key words that fill key slots in one or another of these patterns as a step toward understanding and explicating the poem; for example, in Yeats' "Sailing to Byzantium," to see that the "all" of "all neglect monuments" fills the S-slot of the S/V/O pattern and is not a modifier of "neglect"; similarly to see in Cummings' poem "Anyone Lived in a Pretty How Town" that the utterance "he danced his did" is an S/V/O pattern, in which "did" fills the object slot and has hence functioned as a noun rather than as a verb.

To recognize the chief kinds of lyrics, i.e., sonnets, odes, ballads, elegies, sestinas, vilanelles, and the chief kinds of narrative poems, i.e., ballads and epics

To discern such "sound-effects" as rime, alliteration, assonance, conso-
nance, and onomatopoeia; to judge whether the poet has let sound
betray him into sacrificing sense (what critics deprecate as "bending
the sense to the sound")

To use different approaches, different ways of "getting into" the meaning
of poems — by speaker, by person(s) spoken to, by tone, by key words,
according to the particular poem itself (e.g., in Frost's "Triple Brass"
one way of getting into the meaning of the poem is to start not
with the "Infinite" of the first stanza but rather with the "wood and
granite and lime" of the second stanza — the house-building materials,
which lead the reader to understand that "home" or "hearth" is *one*
element of the puzzling "trio"; similarly the *speaker* is one key to getting
into Browning's "My Last Duchess")

To be able to explicate possibilities of meanings in symbols, but to avoid
premature symbol hunting

To be able to recognize such mythical patterns as dawn–birth–spring,
evening–death–winter, the defeat of the powers of darkness, revival or
resurrection[20]

To identify in a poem the speaker as distinguished from the poet himself;
i.e., to identify the dramatic or speaking voice or the mask, or that aspect of personality which the poet has put on for this particular performance, for this particular role

To recognize, by reading many poems of at least one poet, his characteristic voice as distinguished from the "dramatic" or "speaking voice" he
may assume in one particular poem or another;[21] to recognize, e.g., a
Frost poem or an e. e. cummings poem, or an Emily Dickinson poem

To be able to reproduce from memory at least some memorable lines

---

[20] See Frye, *op. cit.*, Chapter 3, "Archetypal Criticism: Theory of Myths."
[21] In *What Is Poetry?* (New York: Charles Scribner's Sons, 1963), John Hall
Wheelock distinguishes between these two voices and between others. See, especially,
his Chapter III, "The Fourth Voice of Poetry."
Note: Being able to recognize a poet's characteristic voice enables the beginning
poet to criticize his own attempts that may be too derivative.

Habits

To widen one's acquaintance with works of many different poets, and to know a few in depth

To keep a collection of one's own favorite poems; to read them aloud from time to time, and to memorize some of them, if one enjoys memorizing

2. Fiction

Attitudes

To relish fiction; to enjoy the fictional as well as the factual

To respect great novels and short stories as rare and enduring works of art and to admire the investments of time, talent, and hard work that have gone into their making

To resolve to spend more time on the major than on the minor writers

Understandings

To understand that a given master work of fiction (or drama) may operate on several levels of meaning simultaneously, i.e., literal, allegorical, and symbolic, as Dante pointed out as early as 1300 in *The Banquet* I, 1

To understand that philosophic statements and values related to the theme are implicit in, and often arise out of, other levels of meaning

To understand that the novelist and the short-story writer inductively lead the reader toward a philosophical statement, whether expressed or implied, but that this statement need not be — and often is very different from — a "moral" or a lesson

To understand that the philosophic statement in a given work is more than likely applicable only to that particular work itself; that since a novelist or short-story writer is an artist rather than a philosopher, he may not have a consistent or systematic view of life; that, with some few exceptions, it is safer not to assume that the author is a realist, or a naturalist, or a romanticist, but rather that *in this particular literary work* he is realistic, or naturalistic or romantic (for example, compare the idealism of Hemingway's *The Old Man and the Sea* with the nihilistic naturalism of his story "A Clean Well Lighted Place")

To understand the differences between scene and summary — i.e., between dramatic action and dialogue and a narrative-descriptive summation of what has happened

To understand character motivation not only through what a character says, does, and thinks but also through what other characters say and do and think about him

To understand character foils — the author's conscious delineations of contrasts and comparisons; to understand such special kinds of characters as split personalities (e.g., Dr. Jekyll and Mr. Hyde) and *doppelgängers* (Leggat and the narrator-captain in Conrad's "The Secret Sharer")

To understand that a character's behavior in fiction (also in drama) is sometimes unconsciously motivated; to accept a depth psychology as well as a manifest rational psychology as an explanation of behavior; to understand that "depth psychology" may pertain to a character's individual history or to his subconscious identification with an archetypal experience (e.g., initiation or alienation)

To understand that a non-participating narrator or observer, or a minor character in a novel, may be a good friend of the reader's; that some writers (Henry James, for example) deliberately include this kind of character (a "ficelle") to help the reader follow the narrative[22]

---

[22] See Wayne Booth, *The Rhetoric of Fiction* (Chicago: University of Chicago Press, 1961), p. 102.

Skills

To apprehend first of all the manifest and literal (e.g., in *Billy Budd,* after Billy has punched Claggart, Captain Vere and his protagonist try to lift the dead man's body but find "It was like handling a dead snake"), before exploring the symbolic connotations (in the example given above, the symbolic meaning of "snake"); to avoid premature symbol hunting

To identify the setting — time(s), place(s), cultural milieu — and its relation to the meaning of the literary piece; to be able to apprehend all the other factual elements — what Henry James calls "the *donnée*" or "given"

To identify and sort out the *dramatis personae* — who the protagonist is, who the chief antagonist is, who the other characters are and what they are, or at least appear to be

To recognize "round" and "flat" characters (also known, respectively, as "individually developed" and "stock")

To apprehend and be able to reconstruct for the story or novel the manifest story-line — the protagonist's problem or goal, the obstacle(s), the foreshadowing, the peripety or turning point, the climax, and the resolution; to be able to follow flashbacks and the more complicated story lines

To detect central conflict between characters (man *vs.* man) or between man and nature, man and environment, man and society, man and ideas, man and God, man and himself (i.e., one facet of his personality against another)

To discover allegorical levels of meaning — the easiest symbolic, one-to-one representations, which are very close to the surface, the manifest story-line

To determine the *point of view, or focus of narration,* of the "central intelligence" or narrator; to apprehend, for example, whether the point of view, as told in the first person, is that of a subjective, participating narrator (as in *The Catcher in the Rye*) or of an objective, participating observer (as in *The Great Gatsby*); or, as told in the third person, whether the focus of narration is that of a non-participating, "omniscient" observer (as in *Crime and Punishment*) or of a complex of characters (as in *Ship of Fools*); also, to determine the *degree of participation* of the narrator[23]

To perceive how a novelist has used here a scene and there a summary

Habits

To "curl up" more than occasionally with a good novel

To continually read novels and short stories between the reading of non-fiction

To read reviews of novels and collections of short stories (in such periodicals as *Life, Saturday Review, New Yorker,* and the *New York Review of Books*) as one way of selecting books to read

To seek suggestions from one's reading friends in selecting fiction to read

To build one's own collection of fiction, now that so many books are available in inexpensive editions

[23] See James Moffett (ed.). *Points of View: An Anthology of Short Stories* (New York: Signet-Mentor Classics, 1966), especially the "Afterword," p. 566, ff.

3. Drama

Attitudes

To respect drama as an art form to be seen and heard rather than just read

To desire to grow in one's understanding and appreciation of drama

To accept the continuum of quality in drama; to be aware of the fact that there are many plays that may be watched, heard, and read to develop taste as well as for enjoyment

To relish complications of situation and character; to enjoy the rising suspensive action of dramas and their denouements

Understandings

↗ To understand drama as a collaborative art form designed to be seen and
heard, to be produced on a stage with scenery, properties, lighting, and
sound-effects; to understand that very few plays have been intended as
"closet drama" (only to be read)

To understand that *illusion of reality* (credibility) is more important, in
drama (and fiction), than reality itself

To understand that drama began as religious ritual (i.e., rites in honor of
or in fear of divine dispensations) and that many dramas still retain
some of these primitive vestiges (e.g., *Oedipus Rex, Antigone, Every-
man, Faust, The Tempest, Joan of Arc, The Emperor Jones, A Man for
All Seasons, Tiny Alice*)

↘To understand what tragedy is; what comedy is; what a history play is;
to know the characteristics of tragi-comedy, farce, and melodrama, the
comedy of manners and the comedy of humor

To become familiar (once one is well acquainted with traditional types
of plays) with the theater of the absurd — the drama of Samuel Beckett,
Eugene Ionesco, Edward Albee, Harold Pinter, Jack Gelber, Jean
Genêt, and other contemporary playwrights, whose attempts to show
the absurdities of Twentieth Century so-called civilization have resulted
in extravagant symbolical plays, defying traditional conventions of plot,
characterization, and dialogue.[24]

To understand that many master works of drama (also most poetry and
some fiction) operate on several levels of meaning simultaneously —
usually on the literal level and allegorical or symbolic levels (as Dante
observed in *The Banquet* I, 1)

To understand that thematic values in drama are implicit in and arise
inductively out of one or another of the various levels of meaning

[24] See, further, Martin Esslin, *Theatre of the Absurd* (New York: Doubleday Anchor
Books, 1961). A representative collection is *Seven Plays of the Modern Theatre*, with
an introduction by Harold Clurman (New York: Grove Press, Inc., 1962).

To understand the theories of *katharsis* and *empathy* — that by identifying with certain characters and their human condition, by feeling pity, terror, horror, and joy, one purges oneself of certain inhumanities

To understand that the playwright often leads the audience toward a philosophic statement — whether expressly or by implication

To understand character foils (see D–2, "Fiction," p. 42)

To know that *exposition* in a drama is whatever portion or portions furnish information essential to understanding the situation out of which the problem has arisen[25]

To understand the burden of dialogue in drama as both the confinement and the opportunity of the playwright; that the writer is limited to dialogue (plus stage business) in moving his play forward; that this dialogue can be eloquent, witty, profound (and sometimes, alas, banal)

To understand the characteristics and purposes of such different kinds of dialogue as soliloquy and banter or *stichomythy* (witty, "ping-pong" conversation)

To know the classical unities of time, place, and action, and to know also that they are often violated to achieve certain interesting effects[26]

To understand the nature and purpose of comic relief, especially in tragedy

[25] See Fred B. Millett, *Reading Drama* (New York: Harper & Brothers, 1950).
[26] See Robert Brustein, *The Theatre of Revolt* (Boston: Little, Brown & Company, 1964).

Skills

To be able to follow a play performance and to grasp character, motive, and the relationship of one character to another

To identify the setting — time(s), place(s), and cultural milieu — and other factual elements

To identify and sort out the *dramatis personae* — the protagonist, the chief antagonist, and the minor characters

To apprehend and be able to reconstruct the plot (what actually happens) — the protagonist's problem or goal, the obstacles, the foreshadowing, the peripety or turning point, the climax, and the resolution (*catastrophe* in tragedy; *denouement* in comedy); to apprehend the cause-effect relationships which make a play truly dramatic rather than merely episodic in structure

To discern character motivation not only through what a character says and does but also through what other characters say about him and the way they act toward him

To recognize which character, if any, seems to be the author's "mouthpiece"

To detect central conflict between characters or between man and nature, man and society, man and ideas, man and God, man and himself (i.e., man *vs.* one of his traits — comic foibles or tragic flaws)

To be able to distinguish readily between a witty and a humorous character

To detect the various cultural and poetic worlds and stations of sets of characters — e.g., in *A Midsummer Night's Dream* the world of the tradesmen, the world of the young lovers, the world of political authority, and the world of the wood sprites

To discover in certain plays (e.g., those of Edward Albee) allegorical levels of meaning — the most transparent, closest to the surface, one-to-one representations; to discover, also, deeper symbolic meanings

To recognize in drama (also in fiction and narrative poetry) archetypes and archetypal experiences (e.g., ordeals and other experiences of the

journeyer, the initiate, the scapegoat, the outsider, the rebel); to apprehend Biblical and mythopoetic echoes and overtones (e.g., of Job, of
Sysiphus, of Prometheus)

To detect, wherever they exist, the classical unities of time, place and
action; to be able to judge whether they contribute to the play's credibility[27]

To be able to detect dramatic irony

To recognize stock characters; to distinguish between stock characters
and unique characters

To detect, in plays that may be good yet comparatively undistinguished,
deus ex machina (all too convenient rescue of a character or situation)
and other types of contrivance, as one avenue toward cultivating taste

To note foreshadowing, especially symbolic foreshadowing.

To be able to grasp certain structural, lexical, and figurative meanings
from certain passages in poetic drama (especially in Shakespeare —
e.g., "So foul and fair a day I have not seen")

---

[27] In "A Defense of Dramatic Unities" the essayist G. K. Chesterton quipped,
"Everybody knows that the *universe* contains enough spies . . . to kill the vicar. The
drama of detection is in discovering how he can be killed decently and economically
within the classical unities [i.e., limitations] of time and place."

Habits

To attend live theatre-arts performances whenever possible; to choose stage and screen plays of the highest available quality

To grow increasingly sophisticated in one's selection of dramas to watch and read; to continually upgrade one's standards of selection

To read reviews of plays and movies (in such periodicals as *Life, The New Yorker,* and *Saturday Review*) as one way of selecting plays or movies to attend

BIBLIOGRAPHY

Adler, Mortimer. "How to Mark a Book," in *Adventures in Modern Literature,* ed. Robert Freier and Arnold Lazarus. New York: Harcourt, Brace & World, Inc., 1963.

*———. *How to Read a Book.* New York: Simon and Schuster, Inc., 1940.

Austin, Mary, Clifford L. Bush, and Mildred H. Huebner. *Reading Evaluation: Appraisal Techniques for School and Classroom.* New York: The Ronald Press, 1961.

Barbe, Walter, *Teaching Reading.* New York: Oxford University Press, 1965.

*Barnet, Sylvan. *The Study of Literature.* Boston: Little Brown & Company, 1960.

Beebe, Maurice (ed.). *Literary Symbolism.* Belmont, Calif: Wadsworth Publishing Company, 1960.

Booth, Wayne. *The Rhetoric of Fiction.* Chicago: University of Chicago Press, 1961.

Borden, Arthur R., Jr. "On the Reading of Poetry in Relationship to Testing," in *Reflections on High School English: NDEA Lectures of 1965,* ed. Gary Tate. Tulsa, Okla: University of Tulsa, 1966.

Botel, Morton. *How To Teach Reading.* Chicago: Follett Publishing Company, 1962.

Braam, Leonard Steketee, and William D. Sheldon. *Developing Efficient Reading.* New York: Oxford University Press, 1959.

Brower, R. A., and Richard Poirier (eds.). *In Defense of Reading.* New York: E. P. Dutton & Co., Inc., 1962.

Brown, Wentworth K., and Sterling P. Olmstead. *Language and Literature.* New York: Harcourt, Brace & World, Inc., 1962.

Bullock, Harrison. *Helping the Non-Reading Pupil in the Secondary School.* New York: Bureau of Publications, Teachers College, Columbia University, 1956.

*Calitri, Charles. "Macbeth and the Reluctant Reader," *English Journal,* 48: 254–261; May, 1959.

Carlsen, G. Robert. "Deep Down Beneath, Where I Live," *English Journal,* 43: 235–239; May, 1954.

Carroll, John. *Analysis of Reading Instruction.* Chicago: National Society for the Study of Education, 1964.

Ciardi, John. *How Does a Poem Mean?* Boston: Houghton Mifflin Company, 1959.

Clifford, James. *Biography as an Art.* New York: Oxford University Press, 1962.

Cosper, Russell, and E. Glenn Griffin. *Toward Better Reading Skills* (3rd edition). New York: Appleton-Century-Crofts, Inc., 1967.

Daiches, David. *A Study of Literature.* New York: W. W. Norton & Company, Inc., 1964.

Downer, Alan. *The Art of the Play.* New York: Holt, Rinehart & Winston, Inc., 1955.

Dunning, Stephen (ed.). *Scholarly Appraisals of Literary Works Taught in High Schools.* Champaign, Ill.: The National Council of Teachers of English, 1966.

Eliot, T. S. *The Sacred Wood.* New York: Alfred A. Knopf, 1921. "Tradition and the Individual Talent," pp. 42–53.

Empson, William. *Seven Types of Ambiguity.* New York: Meridian Books, 1957.

*Ford, Nick Aaron. "What High School Students Say About Good Books," *English Journal*, 50: 539–540, 545; November, 1961.

Fries, Charles Carpenter. *Linguistics and Reading*. New York: Holt, Rinehart & Winston, Inc., 1963.

Frye, Northrop. *Anatomy of Criticism*. Princeton, N.J.: Princeton University Press, 1957.

Garraty, John A. *The Nature of Biography*. New York: Vintage Books, 1964.

Gordon, Caroline. *How To Read a Novel*. New York: Viking Press, 1964.

*Grommon, Alfred H. "The Curriculum and New Approaches to American Literature," in *The Teacher and American Literature*, ed. Lewis Leary. Champaign, Ill.: The National Council of Teachers of English, 1965.

Highet, Gilbert. *The Anatomy of Satire*. Princeton, N.J.: Princeton University Press, 1962.

Hillocks, George, Jr. "A Unit in Satire for Junior High School," *The English Journal*, 50: 338–340; May, 1961.

James, Henry. "The Art of Fiction," in *Myth and Method*, ed. James Miller. Lincoln, Nebr.: The University of Nebraska Press, 1960.

Jennings, Frank G. *This is Reading*. New York: Bureau of Publications, Teachers College, Columbia University, 1965.

*Lambert, Robert C. "Pitfalls in Reading Drama," *English Journal*, 53: 592–594; November, 1964.

Lazarus, Arnold. "Examination for a Course in the Teaching of English," *Exercise Exchange*, 12: 4–8; November, 1964.

————. *Foundations of Education*, ed. G. F. Kneller. New York: John Wiley & Sons, Inc., 1967. Chapter 5, "Educational Thought in Modern Fiction."

Lefevre, Carl A. *Linguistics and the Teaching of Reading*. New York: McGraw-Hill Book Co., Inc., 1964.

Lowes, John Livingston. *Convention and Revolt in Poetry*. Boston: Houghton Mifflin Company, 1919.

Lowry, Howard F., *et al.* "Literature in American Education," in *Issues, Problems, and Approaches in the Teaching of English*, ed. George Winchester Stone, Jr. New York: Holt, Rinehart & Winston, Inc., 1961.

Millett, Fred B. *Reading Drama*. New York: Harper & Brothers, 1950.

Moffett, James (ed.). *Points of View: an Anthology of Short Stories*. New York: Signet-Mentor Classics, 1966.

Penty, R. C. *Reading Ability and High School Drop-Outs*. New York: Bureau of Publications, Teachers College, Columbia University, 1956.

Perrine, Laurence. *Sound and Sense* (2nd ed.). New York: Harcourt, Brace & World, Inc., 1963.

*Petitt, Dorothy. "A Search for Self-Definition: The Picture of Life in the Novel for the Adolescent," *English Journal*, 49:616–620, 625–662; December, 1960.

Pound, Ezra. *A B C of Reading*. New York: New Directions Press, 1960.

Quinn, Sister M. Bernetta, O.S.F. "Modern Poetry and the Classroom," *English Journal*, 50:590–611; December, 1961.

"Reading with i/t/a," *Saturday Review*, 47:56–57; November 21, 1964.

Reeves, Ruth. *Understanding the Novel: a Seminar Approach*. Garden City, N.Y.: Doubleday & Company, Inc., 1962.

Richards, I. A. *Practical Criticism*. New York: Harvest Books, 1961.

Robinson, Helen M. (ed.). *Sequential Development in Reading Abilities*, Vol. 22 of *Conference on Reading*, Supplementary Education Monograph No. 90. Chicago: University of Chicago Press, 1960.

*Rosenblatt, Louise. "The Acid Test for Literature Teaching," *English Journal*, 45:66–74; February, 1956.

*Sauer, Edwin H. *English in the Secondary School*. New York: Holt, Rinehart & Winston, Inc., 1961. Chapter 13, "Men and Ideas: the Essay and Biography."

*Schick, George B., and Bernard Schmidt. *Guidebook for the Teaching of Reading*. Chicago: Psychotechnics, 1965.

Schorer, Mark. "Technique as Discovery," in *Myth and Method*, ed. James Miller. Lincoln, Nebr.: The University of Nebraska Press, 1960.

Shafer, Robert E. "Methods and Materials for Teaching Word Perception," in *Conference on Reading*, ed. Helen Robinson. Chicago: University of Chicago Press, 1960. Pp. 39–42.

Smith, Nila Banton. *Reading Instruction for Today's Children*. Englewood Cliffs, N.J.: Prentice-Hall, Inc., 1963.

Spache, George D. *Toward Better Reading*. Champaign, Ill.: Garrard Publishing Co., 1963.

Squire, James. *Responses of Adolescents While Reading Four Short Stories*. Champaign, Ill.: The National Council of Teachers of English, 1964.

Strang, Ruth M., and Dorothy K. Bracken. *Making Better Readers*. Boston: D. C. Heath & Company, 1957.

Swenson, May. *Poems to Solve*. New York: Charles Scribner's Sons, 1966.

Walker, Jerry L. "The Structure of Literature," *English Journal*, 55:305–315; March, 1966.

Watts, Harold. *The Modern Reader's Guide to the Bible*. New York: Barnes & Noble, Inc., 1964.

*Weiss, M. Jerry (ed.). *Reading in the Secondary Schools*. New York: The Odyssey Press, 1961.

Wellek, René. *Concepts of Criticism*. New Haven, Conn.: Yale University Press, 1963.

Wheelock, John Hall. *What Is Poetry?* New York: Charles Scribner's Sons, 1963.

Whitman, Robert F. *The Play-Reader's Handbook*. New York: The Bobbs-Merrill Company, Inc., 1966.

Wilson, Edmund. *Axel's Castle*. New York: Charles Scribner's Sons, 1931. Chapter I, "Symbolism."

4

....

Reasoning

Attitudes

To cultivate a zest for reasoning; to accept Socrates' conviction that the unexamined life is not worth living

To believe that everyone's reasoning can be improved

To believe that clarity of communication and clarity of reasoning are interdependent, if not inseparable

To accept the need for providing support and evidence for any assertion or hypothesis

To accept the need for tentative assumptions (working hypotheses) and tentative conclusions

To be receptive to the possibilities, beyond "either/or," of a wide range of hypotheses and alternatives

Understandings

To understand the difference between a statement of fact (e.g., "Shake-speare died in 1616") and a statement of opinion ("Shakespeare was the world's greatest poet"); that is, to distinguish between a statement that can be operationally validated or invalidated from one that cannot

To understand that "operational" or "empirical" pertains to whatever can be counted, weighed, measured, or perceived with the senses; that the term "inductive," often used in this sense, is an imprecise synonym, as is the expression "scientific method"; that the latter embraces both inductive and deductive reasoning.

To understand the differences between inductive and deductive reasoning: (1) that deduction moves from the more general to the less general, while induction moves from the less general to the more general; (2) that a deductive inference or argument is one that is logically determinant or conclusive, i.e., its validity or consistency can be certified by logical considerations alone; for example,

> All women are mortal.
> All queens are women.
> All queens are mortal.

whereas an inductive inference or argument is logically inconclusive or at least requires empirical investigation to determine whether it is true or consistent; for example,

> Ferraris are sports cars.
> Jaguars are sports cars.
> All foreign automobiles are sports cars.

and (3) that the conclusion of a deductive argument is merely an explicit statement of something that is implicit in the premises, while the conclusion of an inductive line of reasoning always goes beyond what is in the premises

To understand the syllogism and several of its variations; to understand that — to use one of the above syllogisms as an example — a syllogism is a formal ordering of three steps as follows:

> *Major Premise:* Women are mortal.
> *Minor Premise:* Queens are women.
> *Conclusion:*   Therefore, queens are mortal.[1]

To understand that even though all syllogisms begin with a generalization or a premise, the hypothesis is the syllogism as a whole[2]

To understand that the syllogism provides a frame for testing whether an argument contains such formal fallacies as the *unwarranted conclusion* (for example, in the above syllogism on sports cars, not all foreign automobiles are sports cars) and the *undistributed middle* (not all sports cars are Jaguars; not all women are queens); to understand that two things which share some characteristics in common may not share all characteristics or be identical in all respects

To understand the "if-then" pattern of reasoning ("If you are a man, then you must be mortal")

To understand the dialectic pattern of reasoning, which consists of thesis, antithesis, and synthesis; for example:

> *Thesis:* X is obviously like Y.
> *Antithesis:* But it is also true that X is something like Z.
> *Synthesis:* Still, X remains primarily like Y or perhaps Y_Z.

To understand why circular reasoning is undesirable; to understand, for example, that if, in answering the question, "Why should X be avoided?" the speaker says, "Because X should not be associated with Y," he has not really given an answer but has only gone around in a meaningless circle

To understand what *non-sequiturs* are and to realize why they are undesirable; to understand, e.g., that the mere starting of a sentence with "thus" or "therefore" does not guarantee that the sentence logically follows or has any connection with its predecessor

[1] See John C. Sherwood, *Discourse of Reason: A Brief Handbook of Semantics and Logic* (New York: Harper & Row, Publishers, 1960).
[2] See H. Gordon Hullfish and Philip G. Smith, *Reflective Thinking: The Method of Education* (New York: Dodd, Mead & Co., 1961).

To understand the nature of valid evidence; that it consists of logical and empirical proofs rather than of mere assertion and analogy; that analogy can sometimes illuminate (e.g., "The superego is like the upper part of an iceberg"), but that all too often not enough specifications match in the two things compared ("Panacea" may be *like* a doctor's prescription" in respect to multiple ingredients, but it is more importantly *unlike* a doctor's prescription with respect to appropriateness for the individual patient[3])

To realize that there are usually more alternatives than only the two assumed in an either/or assertion; that there is often a wide range of alternatives

To understand that some fallacies are less formal and more insidious, and that some are propagandistic; to understand that many emotional appeals are made by proponents of super-patriotism, super-brotherhood, and super-dogoodism, and to know the functions and dangers of each

To understand the nature of the propaganda devices described by the Institute for Propaganda Analysis,[4] such as sweeping generalizations ("sweepers" and "glittering generalities"), "cardstacking," "name-calling," "bandwagon," "testimonial," and "transfer" (arguments by appeal to authoritative organizations)

To understand that all too often trouble begins when a generalization does not fit the facts

To understand that in name-calling, one learns more about the name-caller than about the intended victim[5]

---

[3] *Note:* Many an analogy suffers, as proof, from the fallacy of the undistributed middle.

[4] See William Hummel and Keith Huntress, *The Analysis of Propaganda* (New York: Holt, Rinehart & Winston, Inc., 1957).

[5] See S. I. Hayakawa, *Language in Thought and Action,* 3rd ed. (New York: Harcourt, Brace & World, Inc., 1963), Chapter 3, "Snarl Words and Purr Words."

Skills

To be able to distinguish between statements of fact and statements of opinion

To be able to distinguish inductive (less general to more general) from deductive (more general to less general) reasoning; and to use either or both wherever appropriate

To muster sufficient evidence and instances from which to generalize; to organize evidence appropriately

To be able to relate conclusion to evidence; to test conclusions wherever possible

To know how to distinguish evidence from mere assertions, analogies, and personal opinions; to distinguish evidence from statistical research, for example, and consensus among authorities

To be able to detect fallacious reasoning

To be able to spot definitions and shifts in definitions

To be able to recognize loaded language

To recognize the propaganda device of "testimonial" and the more subtle or hidden testimonials or "transfers" (arguments by appeal to authoritative organizations); to recognize the other propaganda devices listed on page 58 under "Understandings"

To be able to recognize and use assumptions, definitions, hypotheses, proofs, and conclusions

To be able to use the "if-then" pattern of reasoning (p. 57) not only as a mode of persuading in one's speaking and writing but also as a tool for making inferences in one's reading and listening

To be able to recognize *enthymemes* — incomplete syllogisms (p. 57) or parts of syllogisms (for example, "Nice people don't go there") — and some of their implications ("You are a nice person; so you won't go there")

To know how to define one's terms and to stick to these definitions

To be able to choose appropriate grounds for argument (e.g., everyday evidence, research and statistics, documentary reportage, logical proof)

To know how to make appropriate analogies as devices for illuminating rather than as "proofs"

Habits

To think; to search for truth

To cultivate an inquiring and skeptical spirit; to be open-minded enough to reserve conclusions until the facts are in

To reason calmly; to reason before making decisions and taking action

To try to discern writers' and speakers' motives for advocating one or another position or course of action; to ask why a writer or speaker takes a given position

To challenge popular and long-standing assumptions; to go to the sources of knowledge and opinion; to avoid stereotypes; to entertain new ideas

To change one's conclusions where the evidence indicates that a change is warranted

To qualify and bring up to date, wherever necessary, authorities and sources of evidence so as to avoid relying completely upon arguments from superseded authority

To make gracious concessions to opposing and competing ideas and issues

To avoid vague, ambiguous terms in one's argument

To concentrate on issues rather than on personalities; to avoid "name-calling" (*argumentum ad hominem*) to avoid sweeping generalizations ("sweepers") or what propaganda analysts call glittering generalities; to qualify and sharpen generalizations so that they are closer to the truth, to the facts which may have prompted the generalization in the first place

To avoid "cardstacking" (over-emphasizing favorable points while suppressing or bypassing the unfavorable)

To avoid the "plain folks" approach in one's own arguments; to avoid condescending or "talking down"

To avoid such emotional appeals as super-patriotism, super-brotherhood, and super-dogoodism

To assign valid causes and cogent reasons in the explanation of events; to avoid "post-hocs" (e.g., "Right after you came into the room, my books disappeared . . .")

To avoid using circular arguments

To avoid fallacious dilemmas ("either/or" assertions or dichotomized thinking)

To avoid non-sequiturs; to avoid using analogies *as proofs*

BIBLIOGRAPHY

Altick, Richard D. *Preface to Critical Reading*. New York: Holt, Rinehart & Winston, Inc., 1960.

Beardsley, Monroe. *Thinking Straight*. Englewood Cliffs, N.J.: Prentice-Hall Inc., 1966.

Bennett, George K., Harold G. Seashore, and Alexander G. Wesman. *Differential Aptitude Tests: Abstract Reasoning*. New York: The Psychological Corporation, n.d.

Black, Max. *Critical Thinking*. Englewood Cliffs, N.J.: Prentice-Hall, Inc., 1952.

Brown, Roger. *Words and Things*. Glencoe, Ill.: The Free Press, 1958.

Bruner, Jerome S., Jacqueline J. Goodnow, and George A. Austin. *A Study of Thinking*. New York: Science Editions, Inc., 1962.

Burke, Kenneth. *Terms for Order*. Bloomington, Ind.: Indiana University Press, 1964.

*Chase, Stuart. *Guide to Straight Thinking*. New York: Harper & Brothers, 1956.

Cohen, Morris Raphael. *A Preface to Logic*. New York: Henry Holt & Co., Inc., 1944.

*Cooper, David. "Concepts from Semantics as Avenues to Reading Improvement," *English Journal*. 53:85–90; February, 1964.

*Flesch, Rudolf. *The Art of Clear Thinking*. New York: Harper & Brothers, 1951.

Fordor, Jerry A., and Jerrold J. Katz. "The Structure of a Semantic Theory," *Language*, 34:170–210; April–June, 1963.

Guth, Hans P. *English Today and Tomorrow*. Englewood Cliffs, N.J.: Prentice-Hall, Inc., 1964. Chapter 3, "Meaning."

Hall, Lawrence Sargent. *How Thinking is Written*. Boston: D. C. Heath & Company, 1963.

*Hayakawa, S. I. *Language in Thought and Action* (3rd ed.). New York: Harcourt, Brace & World, Inc., 1963.

Huff, Darrell, and Irving Geis. "Post Hoc Rides Again," in *Introductory Readings on Language*, ed. Wallace L. Anderson and Norman C. Stageberg. New York: Holt, Rinehart & Winston, Inc., 1962.

Hullfish, H. Gordon, and Philip G. Smith. *Reflective Thinking: The Method of Education*. New York: Dodd, Mead & Co., 1961.

*Hummel, William, and Keith Huntress. *The Analysis of Propaganda*. New York: Holt, Rinehart & Winston, Inc., 1957.

Langer, Susanne K. *Philosophy in a New Key*. Cambridge, Mass.: Harvard University Press, 1957.

*Loban, Walter, Margaret Ryan, and James Squire. *Teaching Language and Literature*. New York: Harcourt, Brace & World, Inc., 1961. Chapter 2, "Logical Thinking."

*Moss, Sidney P. *Composition by Logic*. Belmont, Calif.: Wadsworth Publishing Company, 1966.

Ogden, C. K., and I. A. Richards. *The Meaning of Meaning*. New York: Harcourt, Brace & Company, Inc., 1952.

Palmer, Osmond, and Paul B. Diedrich. *Critical Thinking in Reading and Writing*. New York: Henry Holt & Co., Inc., 1955.

Quine, Willard. *Word and Object*. Cambridge, Mass.: The M.I.T. Press, 1960

Sanderson, James L., and Walter K. Gordon (eds.). *Exposition and the English Language*. New York: Appleton-Century-Crofts, Inc., 1963. Chapter 6, "Logic."

*Sherwood, John C. *Discourse of Reason: A Brief Handbook of Semantics and Logic*. New York: Harper & Row, Publishers, 1960.

Vygotsky, Lev. *Thought and Language*, edited and translated by Eugenia Hanfmann and Gertrude Vakar. Cambridge, Mass.: The M.I.T. Press, 1962.

Wittgenstein, Ludwig. *Philosophical Investigations*. New York: Oxford University Press, 1953. For an explication (Wittgenstein made easy) see Erik Stenius. *Wittgenstein's Tractatus*. Ithaca, N.Y.: Cornell University Press, 1964.

5

....

Writing

A. GENERAL-BASIC

Attitudes

To enjoy communicating; to enjoy writing well

To believe that everyone's writing can be improved

To be fond of ordering and organizing

To be willing to go through the hard but exciting work of developing control in writing

To assume responsibility for the integrity of what one writes

To desire to write clearly and directly; to take to heart the adage, "Easy writing makes devilish hard reading"

To be aware that one of the enemies of writing is dullness

To accept the fact that in order to have something to write about one needs to read and observe; that if one is limited to one's own experiences one usually suffers from an insufficiency of data; that one needs to study what writers before us have thought and felt, as Matthew Arnold,

T. S. Eliot, and others have said; in short, that one needs to be literate in order to be articulate (in speaking as well as in writing)

Understandings

To understand that communicating (speaking as well as writing) is a three-way transaction involving sender, message, and receiver; that the greater care and attention one gives to all three of these, the better are one's chances for successful communication

To understand that not only one's material but also the audience one addresses helps determine and control what one says and the way one says it; for example, one uses informal language in a personal letter, formal language in a serious poem

To understand that the writer is primarily a speaker with a "speaking voice"; that he is playing a role, for example, of a teacher, or a critic, or a debater, or a persuader, or a leader, or an entertainer[1]

To understand that words are not things; that words are symbols abstracted from — or standing for — things; that these symbols are in short supply in relation to the number of things to be symbolized; that *referents* (the semantic term for things or objects referred to by words) are often not shared in common or simultaneously by sender and receiver of the intended communication; that therefore a writer cannot afford to take too much for granted — he must write not only to be understood but also to avoid, as much as possible, being misunderstood

---

[1] See Walker Gibson, *Seeing and Writing* (New York: Longmans, Green & Co., Inc., 1961) and *Sweet, Tough, and Stuffy* (Bloomington, Ind.: Indiana University Press, 1966).

To understand that even though written language is an imperfect representation of spoken language, writing has its own structures and conventions that often differ markedly from those of spoken language; that writing is or can be *selective* representation — in short, an art

To understand that communications (oral as well as written) are signalled not only lexically but also structurally; to understand the chief syntactic structures, among them predication, modification, coordination, and subordination[2]

To understand that devices for signaling subordination include not only subordinate clauses but also appositives, verbal phrases, and absolute phrases

To distinguish various verbals and verbal phrases; to recognize, e.g., which participles go with which nominals so as to avoid ambiguity in writing; to sort out, chiefly by context, participles, transitive gerunds, and intransitive gerunds; to understand and avoid ambivalent utterances such as "She enjoys swimming, boating, and exciting dates" (Is "exciting" a participle or a transitive gerund?)

Skills

To be able to induce rules and principles of writing from a study of the writing of distinguished authors and from one's own writing

[2] See W. Nelson Francis, *The Structure of American English* (New York: The Ronald Press Co., 1958), "Syntactic Structures," pp. 291–366.

To be able to break rules intelligently; i.e., to learn them first and have a valid reason for breaking them

To be able to use appropriately the kind of inductive development that goes from examples to generalization and the kind of deductive development that goes from generalization to examples

To develop skill in letting the over-all structure and purpose of a piece of writing dictate the selection and patterning of such substructures as paragraphs and sentences

To develop skill in creating appropriate and interesting titles, which is part of the traditional skill of "inventio" (finding one's subject), though titles may well wait upon "dispositio" (ordering one's subject or thinking it through)

To develop precision in written language; to make calculated choices among words and word-groups; to differentiate shades of meaning among alternative expressions; to be able to use a dictionary or thesaurus efficiently in finding synonyms and antonyms

To become familiar with and skilled in using such standard usage manuals as Fowler's, Bryant's, and the Evans'; such style manuals as Sheridan Baker's and Strunk and White's[3]

To develop skill in using both reductive and additive devices wherever needed to clarify the communication; as a general rule, to edit one's own writing ruthlessly, deleting "deadwood" (excess verbiage) and any words that get in the way of clarity and directness

To be able to recognize and avoid "which-mires" (awkward series of which-clauses satirized by James Thurber in his essay, "Ladies and Gentlemen's Guide to Modern English Usage") or to know how to extricate oneself — e.g., by recasting and reducing one or more of these clauses to phrases or appositives; thus one way out of a mire like "In the old town in which I used to live, which was a long time ago, I lent my favorite book, which I lost, which was *Treasure Island*" might read:

[3] H. W. Fowler, *A Dictionary of Modern Usage*, revised by Sir Ernest B. Gowers (New York: Oxford University Press, 1965); Margaret Bryant, *Current American Usage* (New York: Funk and Wagnalls, 1963); Bergen and Cornelia Evans, *A Dictionary of Contemporary American Usage* (New York: Random House, Inc., 1957); Sheridan Baker, *The Practical Stylist* (New York: Thomas Y. Crowell Company, 1962); and William Strunk, Jr., and E. B. White, *Elements of Style* (New York: The Macmillan Company, 1959).

"Long ago in my old hometown I lent and lost my favorite book, *Treasure Island*"

To be able to use a variety of syntactic structures for an intended purpose (for example, if the purpose is subordination, to use appositives, verbal phrases, subordinate clauses); to keep in mind that the most appropriate syntax is the structure that conveys one's intended meaning

To develop competence in using a variety of sentence patterns — such kinds of sentences, for example, as the declarative, the interrogative, and the negative; the periodic and the loose

To be able to combine into one sentence by means of compounding the subject (S + S / V) or compounding the predicate (S / V + V), two otherwise uninteresting S / V patterns — e.g., to combine "Moby was a whale" and "Toby was a whale" into "Moby and Toby were whales"

To be able to combine into a complex sentence two or more otherwise uninteresting short simple sentences — e.g., to combine "Moby Dick was a whale" and "The whale threatened many ships" into "Moby Dick was a whale who threatened many ships"[4]

To be able to combine two sentences into one by embedding into the revised sentence a single-word modifier salvaged from the discarded sentence — for example, replacing the two sentences "Ulysses sailed the sea" and "The sea was wine-dark" with "Ulysses sailed the wine-dark sea"

To have developed skill in using agent-verb patterns; in avoiding chains of "-ations" and "-icities" wherever possible (not "There will be a visitation of the alumni to our convocation" but "The alumni will attend our convocation")

To be able to write logically — to avoid non-sequiturs; i.e., to order one's thinking and writing so that one idea follows naturally from another, such as defining in a second sentence the key word in the first sentence, illustrating or giving an example of this definition in the third sentence, comparing or contrasting the idea with another idea in a fourth sentence; to use trasitional words ("moreover" and "however," for example) and transitional sentences as reinforcement rather than as substitutes for the logical flow of ideas

[4] See Kellogg Hunt, *Grammatical Structures Written at Three Grade Levels* (Champaign, Ill.: The National Council of Teachers of English, 1965).

To be able to write clear, unified paragraphs; to be sure that the sentences in one's paragraph (1) develop the topic sentence or (2) answer the topic question, which a good paragraph raises expressly or by implication[5]

To be able to develop paragraphs through the use of examples, comparison-contrast, cause-effect, time flow (from then to now, or now to then) and space-flow (from here to there, or there to here)

To be competent in following conventions of agreement in tenses, in subject-verb, person, number, voice; in avoiding misplaced modifiers, shifts in person, double negatives, unintelligible fragments

To know how to use parallel structure wherever necessary; to avoid making grammatically parallel what is not logically parallel

Habits

To extend continually one's reading and observing in order to furnish one's mind with subjects for writing

To jot down in a journal or notebook ideas and observations that can be used when one is called upon for formal assignments in writing

To bring order out of the chaos of one's experience; to practice control over one's material — over one's subject, form, and language

[5] See Arnold Lazarus, "Defining the Paragraph," *Purdue English Notes,* 16:5; December, 1962.

To study models; to recognize and study the characteristics of clear, effective, straightforward writing and to imitate them as learning-exercises

To write "scratch copies" as an aid in developing one's ideas before beginning the task of communicating with others

To read aloud what one has written, testing its logic, flow, and euphony

To revise, revise, revise

To proof-read one's revisions

To cultivate self-criticism; to judge one's own writing

To invite suggestions and criticisms from others

To seek a larger audience than one's peers and acquaintances; to submit one's writings to the impartial forum of editors (who are neither relatives nor close friends)

To constantly work toward the imaginative and away from the derivative; toward the original, and away from the hackneyed

To use foreign expressions only when they seem more appropriate or expressive than the simpler, more familiar native expressions; to use them accurately

To be concise, but to prefer repetition to awkward synonyms

To play such word games as crossword puzzles and acrostics in order to arouse one's curiosity about words and if possible to extend one's vocabulary

To write honestly; to subordinate skill in the use of words to the ideas one wishes to convey; to avoid trying to impress others with words one does not really believe

1. Spelling

Attitudes

To become sensitive (preferably before Grade 7) to the fact that communications containing misspellings *look* illiterate

To value correct spelling; to desire to become an efficient speller; to deplore poor spelling as a demonstration of laziness

To believe that almost anyone can learn to spell; that facility in spelling is not something one is born with; that it is achieved only through patient study and practice

To be willing to consult a dictionary when in doubt about a word

Understandings

To understand that comparatively few words are frequently misspelled (many handbooks list "the three hundred," "the one hundred," and "the fifty"); that in these "demons" the errors occur, with some few exceptions, in characteristic places (when "separate" is misspelled, e.g., an "e" occurs instead of an "a" before the "rate"; when "embarrassed" is misspelled, the writer neglects to use a double "r")

To understand that many words are not spelled the way they sound or are pronounced

To realize that many spelling errors result from confusing homonyms (homophones) and words similar in features other than sound

To know the few rules worth knowing on the basis of their few exceptions — for example, " 'i' before 'e' except after 'c' "; "no double consonant when adding '-ing' or '-ed' if the word is generally accented on the first syllable" (e.g., "bénefi*t*ing," "bénefi*t*ed")

To realize that one remembers difficult spellings less by rule than by one's own mnemonics or tricks of associating (e.g., for "attendance," "dance at ten"; for "dessert," "a second helping of 's' "; for "separate," "I'll rate an 'A' if I put an 'A' before the 'rate' "; "there is a 'pet' in 'competition' and 'repetition' "); to realize that the mnemonics that work best are one's own, not those of someone else

Skills

To prove to one's teachers, by accuracy in pretests and by respectable spelling in one's papers, that one has earned exemption from the drills given to those who have not as yet "tested out"

To have memorized (before Grade 7) distinctions among such homonyms or frequently confused words as "their," "there," "they're"; "to," "too," "two"; "are," "our," "hour"; "then," "than"; "sight," "site," "cite"; "affect," "effect"; "some," "sum"; "right," "write," "rite"; "accept," "except"

To have memorized (before Grade 7) the few spelling rules worth knowing because they have such few exceptions[6]

To master the spelling of words most frequently used in one's writing

To develop the supporting skill of creating mnemonics for one's own "spelling demons"

Habits

To keep lists of one's own "spelling demons," together with one's own mnemonics; to throw such lists away after triumphing over the "demons"

To check in a dictionary the spellings of all words one is not absolutely sure of

To develop such habit-patterns (preferably before Grade 7) as "look, write, check" or "say, write, say" or "write, check, rewrite"

To visualize the spelling of words, if possible

To use, in writing, the best word one can think of to express one's meaning rather than to avoid an appropriate word for fear of misspelling it

[6] See Joseph Mersand, *Spelling Your Way to Success* (Great Neck, N.Y.: Barron's Educational Series, Inc., 1959).

2. Punctuating

Attitudes

To accept and prefer the conventions of punctuation and capitalization; but to be willing to accommodate conventions to the special demands of what is being said

To believe that almost anyone can learn to punctuate acceptably

To be willing to accept such non-conventional punctuation and capitalization as are found in the verses of e.e. cummings, Don Marquis, and others

Understandings

To realize that "one writes with one's ear," as Anthony Tovatt has said; that punctuation in part signals intonation (stress and pause) in oral and in silent reading; that punctuation is often more useful when it follows intonation than when it blindly follows rule books

To realize that punctuation-marks signal omissions, joinings, and gestures ("kinesics") rooted in the feelings of the speaker-writer; that readers do not hear the sentence the writer hears in his head as he writes unless there are typographical cues to replace the vocal and gestural cues

To understand that styles of punctuating change slowly; that punctuation rules comprise a code of conventions; that these rules are to be found in such sources as George Summey's *American Punctuation*[7] and in many other handbooks and dictionaries

Skills

To be able to use conventions of punctuating and capitalizing, as codified in handbooks and dictionaries; to be able to follow and apply (preferably by Grade 7) the conventional uses of such major punctuation marks as the period, the comma, the apostrophe, the colon, the semi-colon, the dash, and the hyphen

To be able to note when one has carelessly violated the conventions, e.g., when one has confused the usage of the semi-colon and the colon, the dash and the hyphen (especially in typewriting)

[7] New York: The Ronald Press Company, 1949.

To know how to separate two independent ideas by means of (1) a period and a new sentence or (2) a semi-colon, or (3) a comma and a conjunction

To be able to recognize the meanings signaled by some of the minor punctuation marks — among them, the asterisk, the ampersand, and the dieresis

To be able to punctuate by ear as well as by rule

To be able to recast sentences so as to avoid such frequently unnecessary punctuation as underscoring and exclamation points; to achieve emphasis, for example, by recasting, by using such emphatic verbs as "do agree," "does agree," "did agree"

Habits

To proofread; to read aloud what one has written in order to test whether one has used appropriate punctuation — whether punctuation needs to be added or deleted

To consult recognized style books when in doubt about the conventions of punctuation and capitalization — e.g., the Modern Language Association's *MLA Style Sheet, A Manual of Style* (published by the University of Chicago Press), and the style appendices of dictionaries

To notice the way skilled writers use punctuation

To avoid over-punctuating; to avoid unnecessary use of quotation marks, exclamation points, and underscoring

3. Handwriting

Attitudes

To cultivate an attitude of satisfaction (preferably before Grade 7) in making one's handwriting legible and attractive

To take pride in improving one's handwriting; to believe that almost everybody can improve his handwriting with appropriate practice and instruction

Understandings

To understand that handwriting reflects the person, that one is often judged by one's handwriting

To recognize that legible handwriting is a matter of courtesy to the reader

To realize (preferably by Grade 7) that simple legibility is less distracting than ornate or flowery handwriting and hence more desirable

Skills

To be able to write legibly

To be able to identify (preferably before Grade 7) the chief characteristics of legible handwriting: consistent slant, clarity of line, and absence of flourish and eccentricities

To be able to diagnose the trouble spots in one's own handwriting

Habits

To notice the impression which others' handwriting (attractive or unattractive) makes on you

To take the time to write legibly; to avoid rationalizing about emergencies

To proofread one's writing, correcting one's own characteristic illegibilities

To practice, outside of class, handwriting improvements

B. UTILITARIAN

Attitudes

To respect utilitarian writing tasks; to realize that some of the world's work, as specified below under "Understandings" and "Skills," often depends on one's careful treatment of even the most unglamorous kind of writing assignment (e.g., notes itemizing goods received)

To take satisfaction in the sense of orderliness that is part of efficiently carrying out utilitarian writing tasks

To want to be articulate, accurate, and truthful in even the most common, everyday writing task

To be willing to teach oneself on one's own time most of the conventions of utilitarian writing (notes, business letters, classified advertisements); to respect the preference of most English-teachers to spend the majority of class time on more important matters such as expository writing and the study of literature

Understandings

To understand that computers and other automational devices have not as yet pre-empted the writer's utilitarian chores

To know that writing lists and notes can save time in the completion of many tasks

To know that it is possible for the personal letter to achieve the status of literature; that the principle of rendering in detail rather than just summarizing can be exercised in letters as well as in stories and essays[8]

To know that there are several most often-used styles of business letters: the block form, the indented form, and variations of these forms; and that consistency in these forms is expected

To understand such standard devices of taking notes as outlines, questions and answers, acronyms, and other mnemonics

---

[8] See A. Lincoln Schuster (ed.), *A Treasury of the World's Great Letters* (New York: Simon and Schuster, Inc., 1940).

Skills

To develop skill in writing clear, concise, strategic, and courteous business and professional letters: letters of application, complaint, congratulations, request, introduction, and acknowledgment

To develop skill in writing clearly such brief communications as telegrams, announcements, and bulletins, emphasizing key words (mainly nouns and verbs) and omitting wherever possible such determiners as "the" and "a," and unnecessary modifiers

To be able to write brief, appealing, clear, and accurate classified advertisements; to present succinctly the terms of proposed transactions and to choose appropriate modifiers and qualifiers, if any are needed

To develop facility in making accurate, concise minutes (notes or reports of proceedings, meetings, and conferences); to be able to write first drafts quickly, to capture spoken sentences with a word or two, wherever possible, and to compose revised drafts from such notes and minutes; in short, to make an accurate report of a discussion and of the consensus and actions of a group

To be able to write précis of assigned selections: to note a selection's main points and to rephrase these main points in a few sentences, ignoring asides and details

To become adept at taking lecture notes; to avoid trying to take down details but rather to concentrate on main *ideas, points,* and *examples;* to gain clues for sorting major points from minor points (assuming the lecturer has done so) from the speaker's intonation, facial expressions, and gestures, and from such signpost expressions as "this is especially important . . ." and "even more vital . . ."; to discover one's own best note-taking methods and mnemonics

Habits

To make notes and memoranda; to put ideas down in writing rather than to trust to memory completely; to make accurate written records (especially for income tax purposes if one earns more than $600 a year)

To be accurate in filling in applications and questionnaires

To make lists as an aid in organizing work

To invent one's own mnemonics

C. EXPOSITORY

Attitudes

To appreciate the exciting possibilities of exposition as something not only factual or informational ("how to") but also deliberative (the development of an idea, the defense of an opinion, the explication of a literary work)

To enjoy the play of mind needed for composing provocative thesis statements[9]

To take pleasure in asserting, proving, defending, exposing, analyzing, explicating, re-examining, and re-interpreting

Understandings

To know the forms and techniques of expository writing; to know that "explaining" or "telling how" is only one kind of exposition, that many an interesting and significant exposition develops an idea or defends an opinion or interprets a literary work[10]

To realize that exposition is usually a formal kind of communication ad-

---

[9] See Sheridan Baker, *The Practical Stylist* (New York: The Thomas Y. Crowell Company, 1962), Chapters 1 and 2.
[10] See Edgar Roberts, *Writing Themes About Literature* (Englewood Cliffs, N.J.: Prentice-Hall, Inc., 1964).

dressed to a large audience and therefore usually calls for formal usage and diction[11]

To realize that the development of skills in expository writing does not result from mere quantity or frequency (e.g., writing a 500-word theme a week) but rather from controlled quality, from careful application of principles induced from distinguished models and from intelligent revision

Skills

To settle on a purpose for writing a given exposition or even a paragraph — i.e., to inform, to interpret, to argue, to convince, to persuade; to be able to include a clear statement on what is to be said and how it is to be said

To be able to express one's opinion, in an expository essay, about either an expository or a literary work

To choose a main idea or subject; to narrow it to a topic; to expand the topic to a thesis statement; to stick to this one thesis statement and to subordinate to it related ideas

To develop facility in organizing any paper as a whole before writing a draft; to state briefly the point of the paper; to outline, subordinating minor points to main points[12]

---

[11] *Note:* The chief exception to this general rule of formal tone and usage in exposition occurs in feature stories and the informal, sometimes breezy, articles published in mass-circulation newspapers and magazines.

[12] *Note:* A writer who feels he needs first to write something down — anything at all, just to see what he wants to say — should then make an outline as the next step before writing his first serious draft.

To develop skill in organizing an exposition by making topic outlines, using such conventions as main headings and sub-headings of one or more levels

To develop skill in constructing short-statement outlines as a guide to orderly exposition, using such conventions as proposition or thesis-statement, thesis question, main answers, and illustrative supports

To settle on, then to be able to follow, one logical order (e.g., spatial — from here to there, or from there to here; temporal — from then to now or from now to then); or, if one embeds one order within another, to have a good reason for it and to make that reason clear to the reader

To be able to write arresting opening sentences; to write effective "clinchers" or closing sentences when appropriate to the genre (e.g., editorials); but to avoid formula for the sake of formula

To be able to define the way in which one is using given terms; to stick to one's given definition; to avoid shifting (e.g., shifting from one sense of a term to another sense) before providing the reader with signals or signposts

To be able to cite authorities and quote them in climactic order but to avoid the pitfall of the "testimonial" (the celebrity may not be an authority)

To know how to keynote or briefly summarize a quotation as one of the best ways of introducing it; to avoid unintroduced quotations — a string of "as Smith says" or "as Smith puts it" without first keynoting or briefly summarizing (in a word or a phrase) what Smith is about to say, the point that his words make or illustrate or support

To be able to compose, or to contribute to, a classroom newspaper reflecting both contemporary tastes and one's understanding of a standard literary work (e.g., for *The Odyssey*, "The Ithaca Journal"; for *Life on the Mississippi*, "The Steamboat Gazette"; for *The Ox-Bow Incident*, "The Bridgers Wells Bucket") including editorials in praise of or in protest against happenings and values in the given literary work, feature stories and columns, little satires and parodies of classified advertisements

To know how to compare a motion picture, as an art form in its own right, with the book on which it was based

Habits

To read analytically articles in such magazines as *The Nation, New Republic, Harper's* and *The Atlantic* as models for one's own first attempts at writing articles and expository essays

To keep in a journal one's ideas and reactions to books, movies, people, places, and issues as a means of stimulating one's expository writing

To broaden one's audience; to try out one's powers of exposition in the critical forum of newspaper and magazine columns; to write letters to the editor

To acknowledge indebtedness for quoted and for borrowed ideas; to use quotation marks around quoted material; to avoid plagiarism

To use certain conventions of footnoting consistently in acknowledging indebtedness for quoted or borrowed ideas

To avoid misquotations and irrelevant quotations

D. IMAGINATIVE

Attitudes

To derive satisfaction from writing imaginatively; to delight in the play of mind that informs the writing of imaginative pieces

To accept the fact that writing any of the imaginative genres (poems, stories, plays) is not "free-association" but that, like any other art form, it demands the discipline and control defined in several of the objectives below

To be willing to try one's hand and mind at various types of imaginative writing: poems, stories, plays, and familiar essays

To enjoy contributing to, editing, or producing a literary magazine addressed to one's friends and acquaintances

Understandings

To know oneself; to know one's strengths and limitations as a writer; yet to know that one's skills can be developed by discipline and hard work

To understand that the creative process is partly conscious and partly sub-conscious; that it functions in the writer even when he is asleep, that there is an unconscious incubation period which many an idea undergoes before it "hatches";[13] but to realize that once an idea has become fully developed in one's conscious mind, it almost always needs "rendering" — transforming into concrete details and examples

To understand the *principle of rendering* — i.e., of recreating in selected detail, including imagery and dialogue, rather than just summarizing; that such selectively detailed representation is usually called for in the imaginative genres, with the exception of deliberately expository portions of fiction and drama ("summary" as distinguished from "scene")

To realize that well-chosen models can serve as points of departure for the beginning writer[14]

To know that a poem, unlike an essay, proceeds (and succeeds) more by suggestion than by direct statement and philosophic message; that many a minor poet has sold his soul for a "pot of message"[15]

To understand that poetry re-creates experience, whether beautiful, ugly, sad, or happy[16]

To understand that poetry is essentially metaphor, as Robert Frost often observed

To know that through the ages the most distinguished poetry has elicited readers' emotional responses indirectly through imagery and metaphor — objective correlatives — rather than through exhortation

To realize (as John Ciardi has observed) that statements in poetry must be at least as coherent as statements in prose, though they are often more elliptical and compressed

To know that poems do not have to rime; that there are so few rimes in the English language that their long and continued use in the past has

---

[13] See George Kneller, *The Art and Science of Creativity* (New York: Holt, Rinehart & Winston, Inc., 1965), Chapter 3.

[14] See T. S. Eliot, *The Sacred Wood* (New York: Alfred A. Knopf, Inc., 1921), "Tradition and the Individual Talent," pp. 42–53.

[15] See further, John Ciardi, *How Does a Poem Mean?* (Boston: Houghton Mifflin Company, 1960), especially Chapter One.

[16] See Laurence Perrine, *Sound and Sense: An Introduction to Poetry*, 2nd ed. (New York: Harcourt, Brace & World, Inc., 1963).

rendered them tired if not exhausted; that a rime may often betray the writer into bending the sense the wrong way

To realize that such poeticisms as "o'er," "e'er," "anon," "bespeak," and "forsooth," are hopelessly outmoded for today's poet, except perhaps in jest or parody

To understand that mere narrative discourse or even anecdote does not in itself make a story; rather, that a story grows out of *significant* happenings, especially behavioral changes in the main character or characters; that even a significant happening does not in itself ensure a story as much as the way in which it is told

To understand that certain conventional forms (in the writing of fiction, verse, and drama), far from hampering the writer, help him discover what he wants to say[17]

To understand that in much fiction, drama, and poetry the main character usually undergoes a universally identified experience — initiation, ordeal, discovery, revolt, alienation[18]

To understand that plot-structure in fiction and drama arises mostly out of a character's problem; that there is usually a cause-and-effect chain or sequence for each scene; and that the truly dramatic cause-and-effect chain is different from the chain that is merely episodic, as it is, for example, in a biography or in a picaresque novel; that in the last two genres the story-line is held together only because it is about a main character or two, whereas in dramatic structure, each scene is the inevitable outcome of a preceding scene or scenes

To understand that characterization develops out of the conflict of two drives within a character — e.g., desire *vs.* a sense of duty (the drama of *id vs. ego*)

---

[17] See Mark Schorer, "Technique as Discovery," in *Myth and Method: Modern Theories of Fiction*, ed. James Miller (Lincoln, Neb.: The University of Nebraska Press, 1960).
[18] See Northrop Frye, "The Archetypes of Literature," in *Myth and Method, ibid.*

Skills

To know how to use one's own imagination and experience as ultimate resources in one's writing but to know also how to stimulate these resources with controlled observation — i.e., observation with a purpose

To develop skill in observing and in using imagery, in appealing to the senses; to be able to respond to an assignment like the following: "Go to a meadow, mountain, brook, seashore, lakeshore, river bank, wharf, bus station, railroad station, or airport, and record what you see, hear, and smell."

To be able to write, after listening to a piece of music or looking at a painting, one's impressions of the sound patterns or patterns of color and form and the associations they bring to mind

To develop skill in *rendering* — in *showing* rather than just *telling;* in using *summary,* when it is more appropriate than *scene;* in frequently using *concrete details* which appeal to the senses

To develop skill in rewriting a given piece for various audiences (e.g., small groups of friends, public at large) and in various "speaking voices" or roles (e.g., role of reporter, or critic, or novelist, or poet)

To be able to treat the commonplace in a fresh light in any of the imaginative genres, but especially in the personal essay

To develop skill in writing light verse, especially the limerick

To develop skill in writing well some few verse forms such as the haiku, the tanka, and the sonnet

To develop skill in writing the short ballad, especially the ballad which narrates the experiences of a recent nationally significant person or of a character in fiction or drama

To develop skill in writing dialogue for skits and plays, and for re-creating, in contemporary language, scenes and situations (actual and imagined) in classic and modern literature

To know how to establish very early in a story or play the protagonist's problem or goal; or if the establishment of the problem or goal is delayed, to have a good reason for doing so

To master the art of throwing obstacles into the path of the protagonist's progress toward his goal — especially such obstacles as people and character traits, including the protagonist's own traits (foibles or flaws), rather than mere coincidences and happenstances

To develop skill in writing satires of whatever strikes one as inhuman, immature, or unimaginative

To be able to write a parody of at least one author's prose or verse as a way of demonstrating one's apprehension of his characteristic style

To be able to choose, in writing a serious poem, appropriately formal usage; to apply one's knowledge that formal crispness is achieved by either replacing or eliminating altogether a colloquialism; for example, in a poem about a desert cactus, to replace the colloquial modifier "cockeyed" with the more formal "crooked" or to drop the modifier altogether; similarly, to substitute for the colloquial "Let's pray" the formal "Let us pray"

To be able to draw from critical theories suggestions and possibilities for improving one's poetry and prose but to keep in mind that theory follows (emanates from) created models rather than the other way around

To avoid clichés, bad puns, and such left-handed expressions as "October is the most" and "The freeway takes its toll"[19]

---

[19] See, further, Wyndham Lewis and Charles Lee (eds.), *The Stuffed Owl: An Anthology of Bad Verse* (New York: Capricorn Books, 1962).

Habits

To work continually to improve one's writing style

To submit one's polished and seasoned work, or consult one's teachers about submitting it, to such literary magazines as *American Weave, Approach, Audit, Beloit Poetry Journal, Bitterroot, Caravan, December, Echo, Epos, Fiddlehead, Galley, The Goliards, The Lamp, The Lyric, Motive, Nimrod, Poet & Critic, Poet Lore, Quartet, Showcase, The Smith, Snowy Egret, South & West, Sparrow, Student, Trace, Verb, Voices, Wormwood,* and others[20], most of which encourage new talent; to expect rejection of most of one's early attempts but to keep trying

To copy brief passages of imaginative writing not only to "get the feel" of talented writers' use of words but also to establish a base from which to depart as one develops one's own style

To keep a journal; to make daily entries, in prose or verse, of one's reactions to people, places, events, and readings

To use in a poem, story, or drama, items drawn from the reservoir of one's journal or notebook

To study markets (*Scholastic, Literary Cavalcade, Seventeen*) before submitting manuscripts to an editor

---

[20] The addresses of some of these magazines can be found in *Literary Market-place* (New York: R. R. Bowker, annually) and of others in the *Directory of Little Magazines* (El Cerrito, California: Dustbooks, Box 123, annually). See the latest directories, since addresses change and magazines expire.

BIBLIOGRAPHY

*Baker, Sheridan. *The Practical Stylist*. New York: Thomas Y. Crowell Company, 1962.

Braddock, Richard, Richard Lloyd-Jones, and Lowell Shoer. *Research in Written Composition*. Champaign, Ill.: The National Council of Teachers of English, 1963.

*Burnham, Carter, Jr., Dean Doner, and Charles Green. *The Writing Laboratory*. Chicago: Scott, Foresman & Company, 1964.

Daigon, Arthur. "Computer Grading of English Composition," *English Journal*, 55:46–52; January, 1966.

Diederich, Paul. "The Rutgers Plan for Cutting Class Size in Two," *The English Journal*, 44:229–236; April, 1960.

Douglas, Wallace. "Composition and the Editorial Process," in *Reflections on High School English*, ed. Gary Tate. Tulsa, Okla.: University of Tulsa, 1966.

End-of-Year Examinations in English. Boston: English Commission, College Entrance Examination Board, 1963.

Fogarty, Daniel. *Roots for a New Rhetoric*. New York: Columbia University Press, 1959.

Gibson, Walker. *Seeing and Writing*. New York: Longmans, Green & Co., Inc., 1961.

———. *Sweet, Tough, and Stuffy*. Bloomington, Ind.: Indiana University Press, 1966.

Gordon, Edward J. (ed.). *Writing and Literature in the Secondary School*. New York: Holt, Rinehart & Winston, Inc., 1965.

Graves, Robert, and Alan Hodge. *The Reader over Your Shoulder*. New York: The Macmillan Co., 1961.

Hall, Robert A., Jr. *Sound and Spelling in English*. Philadelphia: Chilton and Company, 1961.

*Hanna, Geneva. "Proofreading, a Panacea: Attention Junior High English Teachers," *English Journal*, 51:482–483; October, 1962.

Harris, David P. "The Testing of Student Writing Ability," in *Reflections on High School English*, ed. Gary Tate. Tulsa, Okla.: University of Tulsa, 1966.

*Hook, J. N. *Guide to Good Writing*. New York: The Ronald Press Company, 1962.

Horn, Thomas. *Research on Handwriting and Spelling*. Champaign, Ill.: The National Council of Teachers of English, 1966.

Jenkinson, Edward, *et al.* (eds.). *Teacher's Guide to High School Journalism*. Indianapolis: Indiana State Department of Public Instruction, in Cooperation with the Newspaper Fund of the *Wall Street Journal*, 1965.

Jewett, Arno (ed.). *Improving English Composition*. Washington: The National Education Association, 1965.

*Josephs, Lois. "A Disciplined Approach to Creative Writing," *English Journal*, 51:468–473; October, 1962.

Judine, Sister M. (ed.). *A Guide for Evaluating Student Compositions*. Champaign, Ill.: The National Council of Teachers of English, 1965.

Kane, Thomas, and Leonard Peters. *A Practical Rhetoric of Expository Prose*. New York: Oxford University Press, 1966.

Kitzhaber, Albert R. *Themes, Theories, and Therapy: The Teaching of Writing in College*. New York: McGraw-Hill Book Co., Inc., 1963.

Lazarus, Arnold. "On the Teaching of Composition," in *Reflections on High School English*, ed. Gary Tate. Tulsa, Okla.: University of Tulsa, 1966.

————. "Defining the Paragraph," *Purdue English Notes*, 16:5; December, 1962.

Lewis, Wyndham, and Charles Lee (eds.). *The Stuffed Owl: An Anthology of Bad Verse*. New York: Capricorn Books, 1962.

Martin, Harold, and Richard M. Ohmann. *The Logic and Rhetoric of Exposition*. New York: Holt, Rinehart & Winston, Inc., 1963.

Mawson, E. O. Sylvester. *Dictionary of Foreign Terms*. New York: Bantam Books, 1961.

Mearns, Hughes. *Creative Power* (2nd rev. ed.). New York: Dover Publications, 1958.

Meckel, Henry C. "Research on Teaching Composition and Literature," in *Handbook of Research on Teaching*, ed. N. L. Gage. Chicago: Rand McNally & Co., 1963.

Mersand, Joseph. *Spelling Your Way to Success*. Great Neck, N.Y.: Barron's Educational Series, Inc., 1959.

Partridge, Eric. *A Dictionary of Clichés*. New York: E. P. Dutton & Co., Inc., 1963.

Perrin, Porter. *Writer's Guide and Index to English* (4th ed.), revised by Karl W. Dykema and Wilma R. Ebbitt. Chicago: Scott, Foresman & Co., 1965.

Roberts, Edgar. *Writing Themes about Literature.* Englewood Cliffs, N.J.: Prentice Hall, Inc., 1964.

Rockas, Leo. *Models of Rhetoric.* New York: St. Martin's Press, 1964.

Salmon, Webb. "Selecting Topics for Composition from the Study of Literature," in *Reflections on High School English,* ed. Gary Tate. Tulsa, Okla.: University of Tulsa, 1966.

Sledd, James. "Coordination Faulty and Subordination Upside-Down," in *Modern Essays on Writing and Style,* ed. Paul C. Wermuth. New York: Holt, Rinehart & Winston, Inc., 1964.

Stewart, Powell. *Teach Them How to Read, Teach Them How to Write* (film series). Austin, Tex.: University of Texas, 1963.

Summey, George, Jr. *American Punctuation.* New York: The Ronald Press Company, 1949.

Tovatt, Antony. "Oral-Aural-Visual Stimuli for Teaching Composition," *English Journal,* 54:191–195; March, 1965.

Walter, Nina. *Let Them Write Poetry.* New York: Holt, Rinehart & Winston, Inc., 1962.

Watkins, Floyd C. and Karl Knight. *Readings on the Craft of Writing.* Boston: Houghton Mifflin Company, 1966.

Wiatt, William. "On Making Theme Assignments," *The Hoosier Schoolmaster,* 4:19–21; March, 1965.

Wilson, Grace (ed.). *Composition Situations.* Champaign, Ill.: The National Council of Teachers of English, 1966.

Wrinn, Mary. *The Hollow Reed.* New York: Harper & Brothers, 1935.

Appendix

....

Language Study
for Teachers

Attitudes

To enjoy language and the study of language; to be interested in many different kinds of speech — even utterances of birds and beasts

To believe that the study of language is rewarding

To believe that everyone ought to re-examine, from time to time, his ideas about language

To respect differences among grammars and grammarians

Note: Some of this section first appeared as "Language-Learning Objectives," in *Word Study,* 40:1–4; February, 1965, and is reprinted here by permission. Copyright © 1965 by G. & C. Merriam Co., Publishers of the Merriam-Webster Dictionaries.

97

Understandings

To understand that language is only one kind of human behavior, only one of the various devices for communicating, and yet so significantly different from all other kinds as to set man apart from the rest of the animal kingdom[1]

To understand that various cultures structure their realities (hence their languages) variously; that to consider the languages of certain other cultures as "primitive" or "less sophisticated" than ours is nonsense; that there is no such thing as a "simple language" or a "highly developed" one; that all human languages are remarkably developed, even those that are only as yet spoken — i.e., even those that do not have a graphics system[2]

To understand that within our Western cultures — even within the United States — subcultures use different, not necessarily better or worse, language patterns; that the degrees of difference, however, are outnumbered by the degrees of similarities[3]

To realize that language changes constantly; that this change is normal; but that syntax (grouping and structural relationships between words) changes much more slowly than do lexical or dictionary meanings of words

---

[1] See John Carroll, *The Study of Language* (Cambridge, Mass.: Harvard University Press, 1955).

[2] See B. L. Whorf, *Language, Thought, and Reality* (Cambridge, Mass.: The M.I.T. Press, 1956), p. 27; also, Samuel I. Hayakawa, *Language in Thought and Action,* 2nd ed. (New York: Harcourt, Brace & World, Inc., 1964).

[3] See H. L. Mencken and Raven McDavid, *The American Language* (New York: Alfred A. Knopf, Inc., 1963); also Frederick G. Cassidy *et al.* (eds.), *A Dictionary of American Regional English* (Madison, Wisc.: University of Wisconsin Press, in press).

To know the history of our language and its relation to other languages in the Indo-European family[4]

To understand that "grammar" is not a set of rules for usage but rather a set (or sets) of descriptions of utterances; that certain grammarians are interested in one or another of the following features of utterances: (1) structure, (2) lexical content, and (3) context

To understand that grammar is one but only one branch of linguistics or language study; that language study embraces many branches, among them *dialectology* (study of dialects), *phonology* (study of sounds), *etymology* (study of word origins and derivations), *lexicography* (dictionary making), *usage* (social, cultural, and regional preferences of language users), and *semantics* (study of meanings)

To understand that a grammar worked out by a particular school of grammarians is primarily a *system* designed to describe characteristic phenomena of language; that all systems, all grammars, "leak" — i.e., their so-called rules do not hold for irregularities and exceptions; that all these systems are artificial or man-made rather than natural to or inherent in a language itself[5]

To understand that there is more than one grammar; that such grammars as traditional-Latinate, structural, transformational, generative, and tagmemic or contextual do not necessarily conflict but are different (often discontinuous) ways of looking at certain phenomena of language; that *Latinate grammar* is concerned more with individual words, especially inflected words, than with word groups; that *structural grammar* (sometimes called *positional grammar*) is concerned partly with inflections and sounds and partly with positions of words in word groups; that structural grammar looks at language particularly as if it were frozen in time at a precise instant and inductively examines certain contrastive features, among them contrasts in pitch, stress, and pause; that *transformational grammar* looks at language in operation, identifies basic sentence patterns and their characteristic transformations; that *generative grammar* (which underlies transformational grammar) looks at

---

[4] See Otto Jespersen, *Growth and Structure of the English Language* (New York: Doubleday Anchor Books, 1948); also, Albert Baugh, *A History of the English Language* (New York: Appleton-Century-Crofts, Inc., 1957).

[5] Most grammarians, unlike scientists in other disciplines, deny or resist this semantic fact of life. Transformationalists, in fact, are willing to apply the description "man-made" only to such an artificial system as computer language. See Owen Thomas, *Transformational Grammar and the Teacher of English* (New York: Holt, Rinehart & Winston, Inc., 1965), p. 25.

language deductively and tries to formulate the rules that will generate and account for "well-formed" sentences; that *tagmemic grammar* looks at both structure and context beyond the sentence

To understand that one grammar or another may appropriately explain certain elements in the language: that structural grammar, e.g., can describe some of the phonetic distinctions between "ship" and "sheep" or between "lighthouse keeper" and "light housekeeper"; that positional grammar (shared by both structuralists and transformationalists) makes sense in explaining a sentence of Shakespeare's which contains an S/V pattern with the S and V far apart or with the S/V inverted to a V/S; that transformational grammar neatly explains the compression in a poem of Emily Dickinson's, in which she has *embedded* in one *kernel sentence* (basic S/V pattern) some other kernel sentences compressed to a one-word modifier; that tagmemic grammar explains the possibilities of meaning in the context of a paragraph; that traditional Latinate grammar explains the sense and style of an ("ablative") absolute phrase or why a Latinist says "Whom are you calling?" instead of "Who are you calling?"

To understand three main distinctions of contemporary English-language scholars regardless of their persuasions as to kinds of grammar: (1) the distinction between *grammar* and *usage*, i.e., that the expression "rules of grammar" is now outmoded in the sense of "correct usage in speaking and writing" — that the term "grammar" now pertains to describing the structure of an utterance, with or without value-judgments regarding its social acceptability, appropriateness, or inappropriateness; (2) the distinction between *cultural levels* and *functional varieties of usage*, i.e., that the old dichotomy of "correct" vs. "incorrect" usage is obsolete[6] — that today usage refers to (a) *formal* or *informal varieties of speaking or writing*, on the one hand, and (b) *cultural* and *subcultural levels* (educated, half-educated, illiterate; national, regional, local or pocket-dialectal), on the other; (3) the distinction between *formal* and *informal functional varieties of usage*, i.e., that the old notion that writing tends to be more formal and speaking more informal is now out of date — that *formal usage* prevails for *formal occasions or functions* of speaking *and* writing, and *informal usage* obtains for *informal occasions or functions* of speaking *and* writing

[6] See Robert A. Hall, "Right *vs.* Wrong," in *Aspects of American English*, ed. Elizabeth Kerr and Ralph Aderman (New York: Harcourt Brace & World, Inc., 1963), pp. 219–228; and John Kenyon, "Cultural Levels and Functional Varieties," in *Readings in Applied English Linguistics* (2nd ed.), ed. Harold B. Allen (New York: Appleton-Century-Crofts, Inc., 1964).

To understand that meanings are signaled partly by utterance *patterns;* that expanded and reduced forms of these patterns occur frequently but that the most frequent basic patterns include (1) S/V, (2) S/V/O, and (3) S/LV/C[7] patterns;[8] to understand that the S/V/O or the S/V/iO/O pattern reflects the drama in which somebody does something to somebody else, while the S/LV/C pattern reflects the metaphor of lyric and essay[9]

To understand equivalent or near-equivalent terms: to understand, for example, that the traditional *dependent* or *subordinate clause* is the *constituent* in transformational grammar, while the *independent* or *main clause* is the *matrix* and may also be a *kernel* if it patterns S/V, or S/V/O, or S/LV/C; that determiners in structural and in transformational grammars include the traditional *articles* ("a," "an," "the") and *demonstrative adjectives* ("this," "that," "these," "those"); that *morphemes* include *prefixes, infixes,* and *suffixes*

To understand that word-groups filling a sentence pattern's noun slots and verb slots comprise the chief building blocks of utterances, regardless of how one dissects these clusters into more immediate constituents

To understand such words (often called "form words") as those that change their forms by means of "-s," "-ly," "-ed," "-en," "-ing," and by means of other affixes; and such words (often called "function words") as determiners and connectors; to distinguish such coordinating signals as "and," "but," and "or" from such subordinating signals as "who," "which," "that," "since," "when," "although," "because," and "if"

To understand that rules and principles of language structure can be induced from specimens of written language; for example, structural signals can easily be induced from the following nonsense (adapted from Lewis Carroll): "It was brillig, and the slithiest toves jyred and jimbled in the shmabe."

To know the differences (whether in traditional or contemporary terms) between independent or coordinate clauses, on the one hand, and dependent or subordinate clauses on the other hand; to understand that

---

[7] Subject / Linking Verb / Complement.
[8] See Paul Roberts, *English Syntax* (New York: Harcourt, Brace & World, Inc., 1964).
[9] See Kenneth Burke, *A Grammar of Motives* (New York: Prentice-Hall, Inc., 1954), Chapter One.

certain structurally subordinate clauses do not necessarily signal logical subordination ("I had only gone one block when I realized my blunder," for example, is a perfectly idiomatic utterance)[10]

To understand that in a simple sentence such as (1) "Ulysses sailed the wine-dark sea" there are really two "kernel sentences": (2a), "Ulysses sailed the sea" and (2b), "The sea was wine dark"; that sentence 2b is "embedded" in sentence 1; that this process of embedding accounts for much of the rich compression ("transformational density") in the works of a poet like Emily Dickinson, as Owen Thomas has observed[11]

To understand that a basic simple sentence ("kernel") frequently "transforms" (a loose but operational description) to a question, a negation, a passive, and (often in poetry) to an inversion[12]

To understand that even though meaning is signaled only partly by lexical content, lexical content does signal meaning — a fact never denied by the structuralists, although they have emphasized the great importance of structure in signaling meaning[13]; e.g., in English, "Horace killed Harris" means something quite different from "Harris killed Horace," whereas in Latin the subject and object were signaled primarily by word-endings rather than by positions

To realize that a knowledge of etymology and the history of language helps one understand literary pieces; that recognizing the various meanings which prefixes and suffixes signal in various situations is rewarding, as is an understanding of doublets (e.g., "guard" and "ward"; "cattle" and "chattel") and of the gallicizing that has occurred in English since Anglo-Saxon times; that language is constantly changing; that guardians self-appointed to keep our language "pure" are deluding themselves[14]

---

[10] See James Sledd, "Coordination Faulty and Subordination Upside-Down," *College Composition and Communication*, 7:181–187; December, 1956. For the idiomatic position of *only* see Robert Pooley, *Teaching English Usage* (New York: Appleton-Century-Crofts, Inc., 1946), p. 92, ff.

[11] *Op. cit.*

[12] See Noam Chomsky, *Aspects of a Theory of Syntax* (Cambridge, Mass.: The M.I.T. Press, 1965); Roberts, *op. cit.;* and Thomas, *op. cit.*

[13] *Note:* Nevertheless, certain contemporary grammarians insist on the priority of structure over lexical content, on the priority of spoken over written language.

[14] See Jespersen, *op. cit.;* Walter W. Skeat, *A Concise Etymological Dictionary of the English Language* (New York: Capricorn Books, 1963); and J. B. Greenough and G. L. Kittredge, *Words and Their Ways in English Speech* (New York: Macmillan Paperbacks, 1961).

To understand that language is an imperfect representation of whatever words stand for; that words are in short supply in relation to the number of things to be symbolized; that words are not things but rather abstractions — symbols for things — which may or may not be arranged in a hierarchy as more or less abstract, more or less general and particular[15]

To understand that language in context suggests meaning — that it often suggests more than it denotes, that it is connotative of what Hayakawa calls "snarls" and "purrs" as well as of intended "neutrals"[16]

To understand that some of the current talk about the "priority of spoken over written language" ("the primacy of speech") is ambiguous if not confusing; that while historically speech did precede writing, the life of the mind achieved considerably heightened development through the development of written communication; that even though we speak more often than we write (just as we breathe more often than we speak), we need much more instruction in the more complex and difficult arts of reading and writing — that, for native speakers, reading and writing have a priority as far as learning and teaching are concerned[17]

---

[15] See Hayakawa, *op. cit.*; and P. W. Bridgman, "The Way Things Are," in *The Limits of Language*, ed. Walker Gibson (New York: Hill & Wang. Inc., 1962).

[16] See Hayakawa, *op. cit.*; and Louis Zahner, Arthur Mullin, and Arnold Lazarus, *The English Language*, *Senior Course* (New York: Harcourt, Brace & World, Inc., 1966).

[17] *Note:* Language *skills* — i.e., applications of the above attitudes and understandings — are listed in the previous five sections of this inventory.

BIBLIOGRAPHY

Baugh, Albert C. *A History of the English Language* (2nd ed.). New York: Appleton-Century-Crofts, Inc., 1957.

Bloomfield, Leonard. *Language.* New York: Henry Holt & Co., Inc., 1933.

Bridgman, P. W. "The Way Things Are," in *The Limits of Language,* ed. Walker Gibson. New York: Hill & Wang, Inc., 1962.

*Bryant, Margaret. *Current American Usage.* New York: Funk & Wagnalls, 1962.

Burke, Kenneth. *A Grammar of Motives.* New York: Prentice-Hall, Inc., 1954.

Carroll, John. *The Study of Language.* Cambridge, Mass.: Harvard University Press, 1955.

Cassidy, Frederic G., *et al.* (eds.). *A Dictionary of American Regional English.* Madison, Wisc.: University of Wisconsin Press (in press).

Chomsky, Noam. *Aspects of a Theory of Syntax.* Cambridge, Mass.: The M.I.T. Press, 1965.

*Davis, A. L., and Roger Shuy (eds.). *Social Dialects and Language Learning.* Champaign, Ill.: The National Council of Teachers of English, 1965.

Dean, Leonard F., and Kenneth G. Wilson (eds.). *Essays on Language and Usage.* New York: Oxford University Press, 1959.

De Camp, David. "Dimensions of English Usage," in *Reflections on High School English,* ed. Gary Tate. Tulsa, Okla.: University of Tulsa, 1966.

Emig, Janet A., James T. Fleming, and Helen M. Popp (eds.). *Language and Learning.* New York: Harcourt, Brace & World, Inc., 1966.

Francis, W. Nelson. *The English Language.* New York: W. W. Norton & Company, Inc., 1963.

————. *The Structure of American English.* New York: The Ronald Press Company, 1958.

Fries, Charles. *Linguistics and Reading.* New York: Holt, Rinehart & Winston, Inc., 1963.

Gleason, H. A., Jr. *Linguistics and English Grammar.* New York: Holt, Rinehart & Winston, Inc., 1965.

*Gove, Philip B. "Status Labels," in "Explanatory Notes," *Webster's Seventh New Collegiate Dictionary.* Springfield, Mass.: G. and C. Merriam Company, Publishers, 1965. P. 11a.

Greenough, J. B., and G. L. Kittredge. *Words and Their Ways in English Speech.* New York: Macmillan Paperbacks, 1961.

Hall, Robert A. "Right *vs.* Wrong," in *Aspects of American English,* ed. Elizabeth Kerr and Ralph Aderman. New York: Harcourt, Brace & World, Inc., 1963. Pp. 219–228.

Harris, Zellig. "Discourse Analysis: A Sample Text," *Language,* 28:474–494; January–March, 1952.

Hill, Archibald. "Grammaticality," in *Applied English Linguistics* (2nd ed.), ed. Harold B. Allen. New York: Appleton-Century-Crofts, Inc., 1964. Pp. 163–172.

*Hook, J. N. *The Teaching of High School English* (2nd ed.). New York: The Ronald Press Company, 1965. Chapter 9, "Grammar(s): A Rationale."

Hunt, Kellogg. *Grammatical Structures Written at Three Grade Levels.* Champaign, Ill.: The National Council of Teachers of English, 1965.

Jesperson, Otto. *Growth and Structure of the English Language.* New York: Doubleday Anchor Books, 1948.

Joos, Martin. *The Five Clocks.* Bloomington, Ind.: Indiana University Press, 1962.

Kenyon, John S. "Cultural Levels and Functional Varieties," in *Readings in Applied English Linguistics* (2nd ed.), ed. Harold B. Allen. New York: Appleton-Century-Crofts, Inc., 1964.

Kottler, Barnet, and Martin Light. *The World of Words.* Boston: Houghton Mifflin Company, 1967.

*Laird, Charlton. *The Miracle of Language.* Cleveland, Ohio: The World Publishing Company, 1953.

Lees, Robert B., and E. S. Klima. "Rules for English Pronominalization," *Language,* 39:17–28; January–March, 1963.

Lloyd, Donald J., and Harry R. Warfel. *American English in Its Cultural Setting.* New York: Alfred A. Knopf, Inc., 1965.

*Malmstrom, Jean. *Dialects — U.S.A.* Champaign, Ill.: The National Council of Teachers of English, 1963.

*———. *Language in Society.* New York: Hayden Book Company, 1965.

Marckwardt, Albert. "Introduction" to *Funk & Wagnalls Standard Dictionary — College Edition.* New York: Harcourt, Brace & World, Inc., 1964.

———. *Linguistics and the Teaching of English.* Bloomington, Ind.: Indiana University Press, 1966.

McDavid, Raven I. (ed.). *An Examination of the Attitudes of the NCTE*

Toward Language. Champaign, Ill.: The National Council of Teachers of English, 1965.

————. "Sense and Nonsense About American Dialects," *PMLA*, 81:7–17; May, 1966.

*McMillan, James B. "Dictionaries and Usage," *Word Study*, 39:1–4; February, 1964.

Mencken, H. L., and Raven McDavid. *The American Language.* New York: Alfred A. Knopf, Inc., 1963.

Moffett, James. "I, You, and It," *Journal of the Conference on College Composition and Communication*, 16:243–248; December, 1965.

Ornstein, Jacob, and W. W. Gage. *The ABC's of Language and Linguistics.* Philadelphia: Chilton Books, 1964.

Our Changing Language. (Phonorecording). New York: McGraw-Hill Book Co., Inc., 1965.

Pederson, Lee A. "Social Dialects and the Disadvantaged," in *Language Programs for the Disadvantaged,* ed. Richard Corbin and Muriel Crosby, *et al.* Champaign, Ill.: The National Council of Teachers of English, 1965.

Pike, Kenneth L. *Language in Relation to a Unified Theory of the Structure of Human Behavior.* Glendale, Calif.: Summer Institute of Linguistics, Part I, 1954; Part II, 1955; Part III, 1960.

————. "Language: Where Science and Poetry Meet," *College English,* 26:283–292; January, 1965.

*Pooley, Robert. *Teaching English Usage.* New York: Appleton-Century-Crofts, Inc., 1946. (Second edition in progress.)

*Roberts, Paul. *English Syntax.* New York: Harcourt, Brace & World, Inc., 1964.

Sapir, Edward. *Culture, Language, and Personality.* Berkeley, Calif.: University of California Press, 1956.

Schachter, Paul. "Kernel and Non-Kernel Sentences in Transformational Grammar," in *Proceedings of the Ninth International Congress of Linguistics,* ed. Horace G. Lunt. The Hague: Mouton and Company, 1964.

Sebeok, Thomas A. (ed.). *Style in Language.* Boston: The Technology Press of Massachusetts Institute of Technology and John Wiley & Sons, Inc., 1960.

Shuy, Roger (ed.). *Social Dialects and Language Learning.* Champaign, Ill.: National Council of Teachers of English, 1964.

Skeat, Walter. *A Concise Etymological Dictionary of the English Language.* New York: Capricorn Books, 1963.

Sledd, James. "Co-ordination Faulty and Subordination Upside-Down," *College Composition and Communication*, 7:181–187; December, 1956.

———, and Wilma Ebbitt. *Dictionaries and "That" Dictionary*. Chicago: Scott, Foresman & Company, 1962.

*———. "Grammar or Gramarye?" *English Journal*, 49:293–303; May, 1960.

———. "Syntactic Strictures," *The English Leaflet* (Special Linguistics Issue, ed. Miriam Goldstein), 61:14–23; Midwinter, 1962.

Stageberg, Norman. *An Introductory English Grammar*. New York: Holt, Rinehart, & Winston, Inc., 1965.

Strom, Ingrid. *Research in Grammar and Usage and Its Implications for Teaching Writing*. Bloomington, Ind: Division of Research and Field Services, Indiana University, 1960.

Temperley, Mary. "Transformations in English Sentence Patterns," *Language Learning*, 11:125–133; Fall, 1961.

Thomas, Owen. *Transformational Grammar and the Teacher of English*. New York: Holt, Rinehart & Winston, Inc., 1965.

*Tyler, Priscilla. "An English Teacher Looks at *Webster's Seventh New Collegiate Dictionary*," *Word Study*, 38:1–8; April, 1963.

Weiss, Bernard J. (ed.). *Language, Linguistics, and School Programs*. Champaign, Ill.: The National Council of Teachers of English, 1963.

*Wetmore, Thomas H. (ed.). *Linguistics in the Classroom*. Champaign, Ill.: The National Council of Teachers of English, 1964.

Whorf, Benjamin L. *Language, Thought and Reality*. Ed. John B. Carroll. Cambridge, Mass.: The M.I.T. Press, 1956.

Wittgenstein, Ludwig. *Philosophical Investigations*. New York: Oxford University Press, 1953. See also, Stenius, Erik. *Wittgenstein's Tractatus, A Critical Exposition of the Main Lines of Thought*. Ithaca, N.Y.: Cornell University Press, 1964.

*Zahner, Louis, Arthur Mullin, and Arnold Lazarus. *The English Language, Senior Course*. New York: Harcourt, Brace & World, Inc., 1966.

Zidonis, Frank J. "Generative Grammar: A Report on Research," *English Journal*, 54:405–509; May, 1965.

Index